Smart Selling: A Guide to Successful Sales Techniques for Bankers

JUDITH A. PENNINGTON
President
Pennington Group, Inc.

Bankers Publishing Company
Rolling Meadows, Illinois

Library of Congress: 89-85813

Copyright © 1989 by Bankers Publishing Company, Rolling Meadows, Illinois. All rights reserved. This book or any parts of it may not be reproduced in any form without written permission from the publisher.

Printed in the United States of America.

No. 970   ISBN: 1-55520-162-8

This book is dedicated to my clients, who have transcended the traditional role of banker to become successful calling officers.

It is with respect and pride that I honor your achievements.

Contents

LIST OF TABLES   *x*
INTRODUCTION   *xi*
OPPORTUNITY INDEX   *xvi*

1 THE SALES CYCLE

The Process of Selling	2
Follow-up	14
Progressing Through the Stages to a Successful Close	14
Selling Intangibles	16
Key Phrases for Selling	16
Ten Paths to Successful Selling	18
Selling Yourself First	20
Package Yourself as a Winner	22
Where to Get Help	26
WORKSHEET: THE SALES PROCESS	28

2 PROSPECTING TECHNIQUES   29

Prospecting from Referrals	30
Prospecting from Published Information	32
Prospecting with the Telephone	33
Prospecting with Direct Mail	34
WORKSHEET: PROSPECTING TECHNIQUES	38

3 THE SALES CALL — 39

How to Get an Appointment over the Phone — 40
Pre-call Planning — 41
Other Elements of Pre-call Planning — 43
Making the Call — 44
Selling Yourself — 44
Opening the Conversation — 46
Call Follow-up Summary: How to Make a Sales Call — 48
WORKSHEET: THE SALES CALL — 51

4 EFFECTIVE SALES PRESENTATIONS — 53

Selling Benefits — the Key — 54
Developing a Presentation System — 55
Key Ideas: A Successful System for a Strong Presentation — 57
Key Ideas: For a Commercial Customer — 59
Sample Presentation Flip Charts for Business Owners — 62
Key Ideas: The Four-Point System for Realtors — 63
Sample Presentation Flip Charts for Realtors — 64
Delivery of the Presentation — 65
Team Presentations — 66
Using Visual Aids Successfully to Enhance Your Message — 67
Guidelines for Using Visual Aids — 69
WORKSHEET: EFFECTIVE SALES PRESENTATIONS — 71

5 CUSTOMER DEVELOPMENT — 73

What Customers Want — 74

Hot Buttons for Businesspeople	75
Hot Buttons for Realtors	77
Selling to Realtors	78
Offer More than Your Competition Does	80
Building Customer Relationships	81
WORKSHEET: CUSTOMER DEVELOPMENT	86

6 HANDLING OBJECTIONS — 87

Objections — Just an Opportunity in Disguise	88
Four Areas for Objections	89
Four-Step Process for Handling Objections	90
Switch-off Technique	93
Rephrase Technique	93
Dealing with Hidden Objections	95
WORKSHEET: HANDLING OBJECTIONS	97

7 SUCCESSFUL CLOSING STRATEGIES — 99

Closing — Just One More Piece of the Process	100
Fear of Closing	101
Emphasize Quality, Value, and Service	102
Laying the Groundwork for the Close	102
Going after Top People with Confidence and a Positive Attitude	103
The Buy Signal: Verbal and Nonverbal	104
The Trial Close	104
Closing Strategies that Get Results	105
If at First You Don't Succeed . . .	111
How to Restrategize When Your Close Fails	113
Words that Sell	115
Words that Alienate	116

Selling to Difficult Prospects 116
The Secrets of Closing 118
WORKSHEET: SUCCESSFUL CLOSING
  STRATEGIES 119

8 SUCCESSFUL COMMUNICATION SKILLS 121

Poor Listening Can Prevent Success 112
Active Listening 123
What Motivates Your Customers? 125
Barriers to Successful Communication 127
Building a Positive Communication
  Style 128
WORKSHEET: SUCCESSFUL COMMUNI-
  CATION SKILLS 130

9 TELEPHONE SELLING 131

Opportunities for Telephone Selling 132
Telephone Selling as a Primary Sales
  Strategy 133
Telephone Selling as a Supplemental
  Sales Strategy 135
When to Organize a Telephone Selling
  Campaign 136
Insuring a Positive Response 137
Getting Through to the Decision-Maker 138
What to Say to the Decision-Maker 140
Sustaining Your Motivation 142
WORKSHEET: TELEPHONE SELLING 144

10 ACTION PLANNING 145

Worksheet: My Major Customers' Needs
Worksheet: Analysis of My Three Major
  Competitors 149

Worksheet: My Sales Action Plan   *151*
A Closing Word   *152*

Glossary of Terms   *153*
Appendix: Success List   *155*

List of Tables

	Questions	9
1.3	The Sales Cycle: Objectives, Skills, and Outcomes	13
1.4	Selling a Product versus Selling a Service	17
3.1	The Sales Call Stages	46
5.1	Getting to Know a Company	85
6.1	Beat the Rate Objection with the System Sell	92
6.2	The "Feel-Felt-Found" Technique	94
6.3	Guidelines for Dealing Successfully with Objections	95
7.1	Closes to Avoid	112
7.2	Handling Rejection	116
8.1	Guidelines for Effective Listening	123
9.1	The Telephone in the Sales Cycle	134
9.2	Five Success Tips for Telephone Selling	139
9.3	Choose Your Words Carefully	141
10.1	How's Your Attitude for Success?	147
10.2	Sales Affirmation	147

Introduction

"If you think you can or you can't, you're always right."

Henry Ford

As banking evolves from an "order-taking" environment to a market-driven industry, many banks are finding themselves lost when faced with the demand for selling and sales management skills. Competitive pressures have convinced bankers that they need to change, and that their banks need to change, but how does one accomplish this change? How can you make people want to sell services and emphasize total relationships, when previously their sole responsibility has been to respond to requests? How can you measure sales behavior? How should you change your structure? What sales goals should you have? How will you know if you've been successful? And most important: How can you keep the momentum growing, year after year, and accomplish a long-term change, both in attitude and behavior? I discussed techniques for creating a sales culture in my first book, *Creating a Sales Culture in a Community Bank*, published by the Bank Administration Institute in 1988.

In *Smart Selling: Successful Sales Techniques for Bankers* I go beyond this strategic view to one specific area: the outside calling effort. Most banks have now made the decision to call on businesses, professionals, and realtors, and this guide is intended for the calling officer who is new to selling or the experienced banker who has never been exposed to a structured approach for sales calls. It will lead the banker through all the steps necessary to build long-term customer relationships.

I have been working with calling officers around the country for the past nine years, helping them make the transition to outside sales. I have worked with bankers who represented a variety of specialties, including commercial, trust, investment services, mortgages, private banking, as well as senior officers and trustees. All of them had one thing in common: They wanted to help their bank by selling more business, but they didn't know how. *Smart Selling* will show you how, from A to Z. You'll learn how to:

- Identify potential customers.
- Sell yourself first.

- Identify the advantages of your bank.
- Identify sales opportunities with current customers.
- Prepare for and conduct a sales call.
- Follow up to develop the relationship.
- Close more business, more often.
- Handle objections confidently.
- Develop a winning sales presentation.
- Use the telephone to enhance your sales efforts.
- Plan for effective time management.

This book is accompanied by an optional cassette tape program that will guide you through the selling process and give you additional ideas and tips. I'll share stories with you about other bankers who've faced the challenges you are facing today.

The worksheets at the end of each chapter will help you organize your thoughts and determine your best next step. In short, *Smart Selling* will help *you* become better prepared to face your market confidently.

Selling is a wonderful profession. Where else can you get the challenge of matching your intellect to a problem, the almost daily thrill of achievement, and the satisfaction of knowing you have helped someone become more successful. That's what *Smart Selling* is all about.

Still, there are many myths about selling that prevail. Here are a few I've encountered in my sales training programs:

1. "In order to sell, I will have to change my personality, and become obnoxious."

   First of all, do you know anyone who has ever changed their personality? Psychologists tell us that is takes seven years to change even one personality trait, so it's not likely that you could change your personality even if you wanted to.

   And why try? The best sales kit you'll ever have is *you*, just the way you are. Successful salespeople build on their strengths and use their personality to help them achieve. They are "themselves;" after all, who else can they be!

You will be the kind of *salesperson* that you are *person*. So don't worry about the horrible transformation — it won't occur. The same strenghts that have made you a good banker will make you a good salesperson: integrity, sincerity, helpfulness, organization, and the ability to solve problems.

2. "Customers will hate me."

Smart salespeople are solving problems for their customers, who are very glad to see them. If you can save a customer time, money, headache, or worry, why wouldn't he be glad to see you?

It's only salespeople who push *products*, rather than sell *solutions*, who have trouble getting in the door. There isn't a businessperson alive who doesn't want to see his or her business prosper.

3. Salespeople are born, not made.

This is probably the most insidious myth there is, because it is a mask for the fear: "I won't be able to do it."

There isn't anything you can't do if you want to, if it is within the realm of human capacity and your capabilities. Selling is simply building a relationship with another person for the mutual benefit of both of you. You've been doing that in banking for years. Very few bankers who are succeeding at outside calling answered "Salesperson!" when asked "What do you want to be when you grow up?"

The real challenges of selling have little to do with aptitude and almost everything to do with one's attitude about selling. If you see yourself as a helper, you will be successful. If you see yourself as an intruder, you will have difficulty.

Effective selling requires absolute clarity of purpose — an ability to keep mentally focused on the *end result* the customer's commitment, or the sale — while discussing the *means*. When your objective is clear, you are convincing, certain, and positive. By expecting the prospect to buy, you create an environment for your success.

Smart selling takes both ability and willingness, and you certainly have the ability. Willingness may be another story. But if you want to make the transition, you can, because selling is a logical process with six clearly defined steps. If you apply this system for success, you will be successful.

The average sale is made on the fifth try, and yet only 5 percent of all salespeople persist long enough to succeed. Often the only difference between a failure and a success is that the success tried one more time. It takes persistence to be effective because our prospects already have a bank. So we are dealing with habit. Most companies have been doing business with their bank for seven to ten years, so we've got to give them a good reason to change.

The ideas and techniques you'll read about in *Smart Selling* will help you become more successful, if you'll just put them into practice. The accompanying cassette tapes and worksheets at the end of each chapter will help you get started. If you have the cassette program, please listen to the Introduction on Tape 1, Side 1, before continuing with your reading.

Good luck and good selling!

SMART SELLING: OPPORTUNITY INDEX

If you are...

- Wondering how to get the customer to TALK, see pp. 6–10.
- Wondering how to get a TERRITORY organized, see pp. 29–34.
- Wondering how to get an APPOINTMENT, see p. 40.
- Concerned about how to ASK for the business, see p. 6–18 and pp. 100–114.
- Eager to present yourself as a WINNER, see pp. 20–25.
- Puzzled about how to OPEN the conversation on a sales call, see p. 45.
- Having problems organizing your PRESENTATION, see pp. 4-4 — 57–62.
- Nervous about using VISUAL AIDS for an important presentation, see pp. 68–72.
- Wondering what will get a BUSINESS OWNER'S attention, see pp. 75–77.
- Curious about how to distinguish yourself when calling on REALTORS, see pp. 80–81.
- Have problems answering OBJECTIONS, see pp. 90–94.
- Afraid of REJECTION, see p. 116.
- Eager to improve your LISTENING skills, see pp. 122–125.
- Looking for a TELEPHONE selling system, see pp. 133–134.
- Looking for an ACTION PLAN for the next 30 days, see p. 151.

1 The Sales Process

The way to acquire enthusiasm is to believe in what you are doing and in yourself, and to want to get something definite accomplished. Enthusiasm will follow as night the day.

Dale Carnegie

When you were first asked to become a salesperson for your bank, you probably didn't know what to expect. After all, outside calling is a very different job from the traditional banking relationship where the customer comes to you. And yet there are many similarities. A smart salesperson is a helper, an advisor to businesspeople, showing them how to improve their businesses. That helping process is what bankers have always done so well for their customers. Now you're asked to go out and find the business. It's the same process, but from a different perspective.

If you talk with businesspeople around the country, they all have the same criteria for a banker: someone who understands their business, cares about their problems, and can recommend solutions. No one needs a bank; there are many banks on every street corner in America. What businesspeople need is a banker. And that's where you come in—ready, willing, and eager to help.

THE PROCESS OF SELLING

There's nothing mysterious about selling. It is a process that occurs, a relationship you build with your customer. The success of the sales process depends on many factors, including your ability to present your services favorably, your skill in determining the customer's needs, the relationship you achieve with your customer, and several factors not related to you, such as the company's budget, the economy, the organizational structure, and brand preferences.

The selling process, or the sales cycle, has six distinct stages

1. Identify: Decide who might need your services.
2. Qualify: Narrow that list down to who is likely to do business with you.
3. Define needs: Identify their financial requirements and what they're looking for in a bank.

THE SALES PROCESS 3

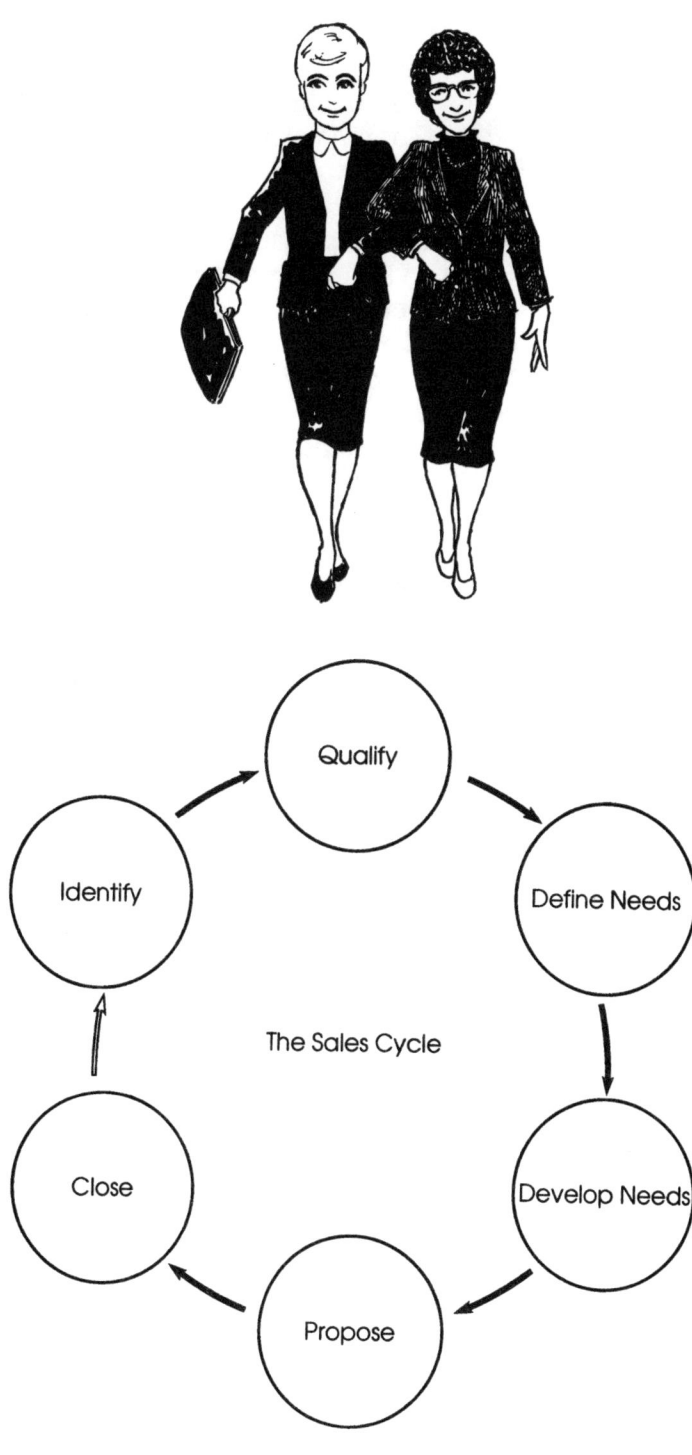

The Sales Cycle

4. Develop needs: Match those requirements and needs to your offerings.
5. Propose: Recommend a plan of action.
6. Close: Ask for a commitment.

Step 1: Identify

The Identify Stage occurs when you begin to determine who the prospects—or potential customers—are for your services. A prospect is anyone who could have a use for your services. At this point you do not know if they are interested or if your service fits their needs. You have only determined potential candidates to become bank customers. For example, as you identify candidates, you would probably list the manufacturing and retail businesses, realtors, attorneys, doctors, CPAs, and other professionals in your area. A prospect list is your list of potential bank customers. By keeping this list constantly updated, you will have a steady stream of potential customers.

A typical prospect list looks like this:

Name	Company	Address	Phone No.
Mr. Joe Smith	ABC Realty	5 Main St. Yourtown, USA	(203) 534-8765
Mr. Jim Bigelow	Corner Deli	16 South St. Yourtown, USA	(203) 354-0098
Ms. Joan Motta	James Mfg.	7 Strait St. Yourtown, USA	(203) 543-0606
Mr. Kyle Botts	WordPro	23 West St. Yourtown, USA	(203) 435-7053
Ms. Susan Or	Hanks, Mancuso and White	15 Sun Blvd. Yourtown, USA	(203) 345-0932

Often the best place to look for potential customers is in your own customer base. More ideas about finding prospects are discussed in Chapter 2. A good prospect list has at least twenty five names, addresses, telephone numbers, and key contacts.

Step 2:
Qualify

Once you have an initial prospect list, you'll use qualification to narrow it to include only those prospects who

1. Have a need for your services.
2. Will consider your bank.
3. Can satisfy the requirements for the service—such as meeting the minimum number of employees for a payroll service or satisfying the credit guidelines.

In other words, you need a few prospects to focus your attention on, and you want to work with the ones you think have the most immediate chance of doing business with you.

The Qualify Stage helps the banker narrow the prospect list to an *active prospect list*, or a group of potential customers to whom you now apply your efforts. At least ten active prospects is a good starting point.

The term "qualified prospect" means that the person is a likely candidate for doing business with your bank. Qualification of a prospect may take place over the telephone or during the course of several appointments with a prospect. The most efficient qualification occurs over the telephone before you schedule an appointment. However, you often cannot get all the information you need over the phone and may make the decision to call on the prospect to further qualify.

If you have no information on which to base a decision about whom to target first, then just narrow your prospect list by geography, type of industry, Chamber of Commerce membership—or some arbitrary grouping you are comfortable with.

The skill required for qualification of a prospect is questioning. You must ask your prospect questions to find out if he is indeed a candidate for your services and is willing to consider a change. This questioning should not seem like aggressive interrogation; it should allow the prospect to reveal information at his own pace.

Once you have a qualified prospect, the next step is to schedule an appointment with that potential customer. Surveys show that at least 70 percent of all businesspeople require you to have an appointment to see them. How to get an appointment over the phone is discussed in Chapter 3.

Step 3: Define Needs

The objective of an initial appointment with a qualified prospect is to identify his needs, concerns, objectives, and special problems. The most important skills during this stage are questioning, active listening, and observing.

The open question. Open questions allow your potential customer to reveal useful information to you. An open question cannot be answered by a simple yes or no; it generally begins with the word "How," "When," or "What." An open question allows the customer to open up and talk to you about his business. And that's how you find out what he needs, so you can begin to think about your solution. An example of a good open question is, "What are your financial objectives?"

On the other hand, "Are you satisfied with you current bank?" is a closed question, and a poor choice too. If the answer is "Yes," where do you go from there? If the answer is "No," you still have to ask *another question* to find out why.

You can assume that a business already has a bank and that they may not immediately tell you if they are unhappy. They may fear that it makes them look stupid to be doing business at a bank where they're not happy. Also, a business owner may not even know if the firm is happy with its bank, preferring to stay out of such details.

The closed question "Are you satisfied with your current bank?" can only be answered yes or no and may preclude the opportunity for you to cross-sell the services your bank offers. Try instead, "What's important to you in a bank?"

Other good open questions include, "How's business?" and "What are your objectives?" These give the prospect the opportunity to organize and reveal information in a way that is relevant to him, which gives you the information you need later to ask him to make a change. (Other examples of open questions are listed in Tables 1.1 and 1.2.)

If you ask these open questions and then listen, you will learn everything you need to know in order to make product and service recommendations.

Directive & Reflective Questions. Directive questions are designed to get specific and precise information, such as "How do you expect to obtain funds for repayment?" or " How soon do you need the cash?" However, directive questions can seem like interrogation to your customer if you ask too many of them in a row or they are delivered harshly.

Another type of question that is useful for gaining information is the reflective question, which leads the customer to reflect on his previous statement and enhance it with clarification or additional information. A reflective question sounds like this: "You mentioned that

Table 1.1. Open Questions: Your Success Tool.

"How satisfied are you with..."
"How are you currently...?"
"Why do you like...?"
"Why do you think of...?"
"What do you like about...?"
"What are your thoughts on...?"
"What effect would...have?"
"What would you expect from me as your banker?"
"What would I have to do to get your business?"
"Can you tell me what you like or dislike about the...you are now using?"
"When are you planning to...?"
"When you think of a bank, what kind of things do you look for?"
"Oh? Can you give me an example?"
"Oh? Can you tell me a little more about it?"
"Oh? What kind do you use?"
"Really? That's very interesting. Please tell me more."
"Do you ever have a need for...?"
"Oh? How does it help you?"
"I'm sure interested in knowing why you feel that way."

Table 1.2. Examples of the Three Types of Questions.

Open	"What are your objectives?"
	"How is your operation changing?"
	"How do you manage your working capital now?"
Directive	"How soon do you need the cash?"
	"What services would you like to have that you don't have now?"
	"How much do you plan to deposit?"
Reflective	"You mentioned that financial security was important. What does financial security mean to you?"
	"It sounds like you're not convinced that the savings would be that great. How can I make you feel more comfortable with the numbers?"
	"I know you want value. What can we do to give you that value?"

financial security was important to you. Could you tell me a little more about that?"

Reflective questions allow you to find out more. For example, if someone says he wants a good rate, what does that mean? Will a passbook account suffice? Or should you be talking about mutual funds? Words like "security," "value," "convenience," and "good deal" mean little if you do not find out what the *prospect* means by them.

Guidelines for Asking Questions. Skill in questioning depends upon how you deliver the question and how well you observe your customer's reactions. Here are a few rules to follow:

1. Start by thinking through what it is you want to find out. There are six basic things you'll want to know about each prospect:

    - Will they consider a change?
    - Do you have the services they need?

- Does the company profile—size, number of employees, method of doing business, credit history, etc.—fit in with the kind of business you want?
- Who is the decision maker?
- How soon will they be making a decision?
- What is the critical factor that would make them change banks?

2. Ask your questions at a pace that does not overwhelm your customer.

    Even though *you* know where you are going, give the prospect plenty of time to think and reflect. Do not be too eager to dominate the conversation. In the early stages of the sales call the banker should be doing only 20 percent of the talking.

3. Next, listen to the answers and observe your customer's behavior.

    When you ask about their willingness to change, does the prospect shift uncomfortably? When you mention that you are doing business with Acme down the street, did she lean forward in her seat as if to say, "Tell me more"?

4. If a follow-up question is needed, ask it to get more information.

    Just because you ask a good question doesn't mean you will get the information you want. Our language is not precise, and your prospect may not understand your question, may not know the answer to your question, may be thinking along different lines, or may just be unwilling to tell you.

5. If your customer seems uncomfortable with your line of questioning, try a new subject.

    You cannot ever build a good relationship with a prospect by annoying him. Remember that you are a visitor in his office and not there by any right.

Occasionally you may sense that it is time to put an end to the conversation. Thank your customer for his time, exit politely, and send a follow-up letter. Although it is rare for someone who has granted you an appointment to be difficult to talk to, if it happens, don't take it personally. Just move on to your next prospect.

Step 4: Develop Needs

In this stage your objective is to find out in more detail the prospect's needs to that you can match them to your offerings. Your skills of questioning, active listening, and observing are still important, as well as the skill of clarification; that is, making sure that you understand the customer's needs from his perspective. The relationship you build with your customer at this stage usually determines the tone of your future dealings.

If you are responsive in providing information and show a genuine interest in his needs, he will probably trust you and respect your advice. If, however, you do not listen to your customer's description of his problems and needs and quickly try to steer him to a financial plan that does not meet his needs, you probably won't have a successful long-term relationship. It is important for you to begin designing a financial solution with your customer in such a way as to avoid pressuring him and to instill his trust in you. The outcome of the Develop Needs Stage is the proposal.

Step 5: Propose

During the Propose Stage, the banker formally presents the recommended financial plan to the customer. The proposal may be accompanied by a presentation to the key decision maker.

Whatever form your proposal takes, it should be written professionally and include the following items:

1. A brief introduction demonstrating your knowledge of the situation and describing your recommendation and its benefits to the customer. This introduction should be separate from the cover letter and directly attached to the proposal, so that all those who review the proposal will see it.
2. A list of recommended services.
3. The effective interest rate, annual yield projections, expected cost savings, and any other financial justifications.

4. Instructions about how the customer executes the financial plan, such as "Sign, date, and return by June 1 to James Smith."
5. Contractual details or the contract itself.

Often the proposal is presented following a formal presentation to the key decision-makers. In this case your presentation skills, active listening skills, and ability to think on your feet are key. A presentation is most effective when it is an interactive two-way process. Your presentation should be designed to cover the banking service features and benefits that are important to your customer and should not be delivered as a speech. A presentation is a two-way communication process; a speech is one-way.

To make your presentation an interactive process, involve the prospect early on with specific questions. When making a point you know to be of interest to one member of the audience, make a statement like, "Alice, I know this is a hot button for you."

You must know what you want to say well enough to be able to change course if your prospect asks a question or gives you additional information. You want to involve the customer and keep him or her interested. So look for these questions and be prepared to be flexible in your delivery. More tips on how to prepare for and deliver your presentation will be discussed in Chapter 6.

The outcome of the Propose Stage is your prospect's agreement on your recommended solution.

Step 6: Close The objective of the Close Stage is to secure the customer's commitment and make the sale. The skill required is the ability to ask for the order. Many competent salespeople go through all the previous stages successfully and yet can never seem to get the last question out: "Can we get started today?" Generally it's just a matter of practice in actually asking the question. If you have progressed successfully through the previous five stages, you will be in a positive position to achieve the sixth. (See Table 1.3).

TABLE 1.3 The Sales Cycle: Objectives, Skills, and Outcomes.

Stage	Objective	Skill	Outcome
Identify	Determine potential Buyers	Research Integration of information	Prospect list
Qualify	Focus on likely buyers	Questioning	Active list
Define	Discover business needs	Questioning Active listening Observation	Account plan
Develop	Match needs to offerings	Questioning Active listening Clarification Integration	Proposal
Propose	Gain agreement for solution	Presentation Writing skills Active listening	Agreement
Close	Commitment to buy	Asking for the order	Sale

FOLLOW-UP

Once a customer says yes, it may be the end of the sales cycle, but it is the *beginning* of the relationship.

Holding on to a customer is at least as tough as getting him in the first place. There are many other financial services providers who will continue to try to get *your* customer to become *their* customer. So be sure to follow up with a thank-you note, additional information, and periodic check-backs to be sure they are satisfied with the service. What you do for your customer *after* the sale will determine your ultimate success. You are in a service business, and providing service to your customers never ends. Your follow-up will create customer loyalty, reinforce the customer's decision, prevent "buyer's remorse," and show your professionalism. And that's how you get references from satisfied customers.

PROGRESSING THROUGH THE STAGES TO A SUCCESSFUL CLOSE

Every professional sale is made by moving through the sales cycle with your customer. It may take thirty minutes, three weeks, three months, or three years, but the process remains the same. The biggest misconception new salespeople have is that they are supposed to go through the door, talking about products and making recommendations, before they know what the prospect needs.

This is the opposite of being a consultant or advisor to your customer. You must first understand what they need and what their situation is before you propose anything. You can probably assume certain needs based upon your knowledge of other similar customers, but you still will want to check it out with each prospect.

The sales cycle does not always flow smoothly from Identify to Close, but there are many things you can do to facilitate the process and build in success.

THE SALES PROCESS

Recognize the Process as a Cycle

We call the sales process a cycle because to make a sale, you must go through certain steps in a specific order, and the process is repeated with each sale. The same steps—identify, qualify, define needs, develop needs, propose, and close—are required for each selling situation. If you can begin to view selling as a cycle with distinct steps, you will be more organized in your approach and will have a better chance of getting the sale. Also, if you are unsuccessful with a prospect, it is often helpful to review the cycle and consider what went wrong. You may find that the prospect was never qualified to begin with; perhaps he preferred to stay with "Brand X" or felt that your product did not really meet his needs.

Understand the Objectives of Each Stage

There's a reason and an objective for each stage in the sales cycle. Although your primary objective as a salesperson is to close (Step 6), you need to focus on the preliminary objectives that lead to that sale. Your skill at achieving the preliminary objectives determines your ability to make the sale. (see Table 1.3).

Focus on the Skills Required for Each Stage

Each step in the sales cycle builds on the skills in the previous step. It will be easier for you to make the sale if you think in terms of calling on additional skills as you go through the cycle.

Keep Organized

When you only have one prospect, it's easy to remember key facts. But when you have twenty-five prospects and fifty active customers, it's not so easy. And yet, giving personal service means remembering accurately the facts about each account. Develop a record-keeping system for yourself. Make notes about conversations and meetings with your customers and refer to them in tailoring your recommendations. Get the correct spelling of names, and keep a chronological log of contacts.

Recognize Where You Are in the Cycle

It is important for you to be aware of where you are in the sales cycle with each prospect. If you begin to think of selling as a process with distinct stages, it will be easy for you to identify which stage you are in. Also, in dealing with several prospects, it will help you to distinguish between them as you anticipate future sales. It is difficult to forecast your sales if you are unsure about where you stand with a customer.

Recognize Where Your Customer Is in the Sales Cycle

Success in selling depends also on knowing where the *customer* is in the sales cycle. The salesperson may attempt to close, only to discover that the customer is still confused about how your service may be beneficial. Staying attuned to your customer is critical at all stages. You must be flexible enough to guide the sales effort and yet be responsive to where the customer wants to go.

Set the Stage for the Sale and Put Yourself in Charge

A successful salesperson begins setting the stage for the sale from the day he or she is given sales responsibility. From then on, all activities are engineered to cause the customer to commit to your bank's services. The salesperson knows that he or she has control over this process and begins to weave the elements that go into making a sale to achieve this purpose. The salesperson—not the customer—is in charge of the sales process. The salesperson's job is to guide the customer in reaching a decision that is mutually beneficial.

This positive control is achieved through the adoption of an attitude of success, backed up by product knowledge and a thorough understanding of the customer's needs.

SELLING INTANGIBLES

The sale of financial services is different from the sale of a lawnmower, which can be felt and touched. With financial products, satisfaction comes *after* the sale. Table 1.4 shows the difference between selling a product and selling a service.

KEY PHRASES FOR SELLING

Selling is often a matter of choosing the right words. What you are trying to do is paint a picture in the cus-

Table 1.4. Selling a Product versus Selling a Service.

Product	Service
Visible	I can't see it.
Tangible	I can't touch it
Benefits obvious	Benefits must be made obvious
Product quality is key	People quality is key
Short sales cycle	Long sales cycle
Customer satisfaction upon delivery	Customer satisfaction over time
Product differentiation by sight	Differentiation by feel
Sales tactic: Show it, touch it, use it	Sales tactic: Create a vision of success
Sales tactic: Try it	Sales tactic: Reference selling
Very little follow-up	Follow-up extremely important
Major responsibility: explanation (before the sale)	Major responsibiltiy: service (after the sale)
Potential for add-on products is 50/50	Potential for account development is high
Customer buys product	Customer buys you.

tomer's mind of how he'll be better off as a result of doing business with you. Here are a few suggested phrases. Try them out with your prospects.

"Would you be willing to...?"

"Many of our customers have found..."

"What would I have to do to become your banker?"

"I'm sure you still have questions. Let's make a list of them. Let's go over each and I'll give you all the information you need to make a decision."

"I hear you focusing on price, but isn't value what you really want?"

"I'm sure you'd like to think it over. Let's pool our resources—two heads are better then one."

"If I can show you how you can get all those services you believe you're entitled to, would you begin banking with me today?"

"We can consolidate and coordinate your needs to increase your efficiency and leave you more time for decision-making and planning."

"Most of our customers have shopped around and they chose us."

"I have a Super Account myself, and I find the advantages are really worth the cost."

"Sometimes borrowing money can get you more than cash alone can."

"If you want to pay for full research, shouldn't you be dealing with our Trust Department?"

"Wouldn't you agree that you'd like to bank with the best bank in our city?"

"You deserve special treatment."

"I'll be your primary contact, and you'll still have access to other talents in the bank."

"What can the bank do to improve your present financial position?"

TEN PATHS TO SUCCESSFUL SELLING

1. Cultivate a Positive Attitude.
The only one who can defeat you is you. Your attitude is the single most important thing you wear to work each day. Make sure yours is working for you.

2. Adopt a Professional Outlook.

Selling is a profession in which you get to help hundreds of people become more successful in their lives and in their businesses. Looked at that way, selling is a natural extension of the good customer service you've always provided as a banker.

3. Preserve an Eagerness to Learn.

The best salespeople are always learning. There is a wealth of information out there in seminars, tapes, magazines, and books. Keep yourself informed so that you will be the best possible advisor for your customers.

4. Prepare a Well-Organized Sales Plan.

Don't just come in on Monday morning and wonder what to do during the week. You are running a small business—your territory—and you'll need a business plan. Plan for next week on *this* Friday. Plan for tomorrow *today*. Don't be caught aimlessly wandering about the office, responding to emergencies and crises.

5. Conduct a Continuous Prospecting Campaign.

To be assured of a steady stream of sales, you always have to be on the lookout for new people to add to your prospect list. Chapter 2 will show you where to find those prospects.

6. Perfect Meticulous Account Management.

Contrary to a popular myth, the most successful salespeople are highly organized. They run their territory by their calendar and have developed recordkeeping and follow-up systems to help them stay abreast of their customers. When a customer calls, the file is within reach and the salesperson can respond personally to the request.

7. Practice Presentation Skills.

When a group of decision-makers, a firm of realtors, or a board of directors asks you to present your ideas, make sure that you shine. Good presentations are just a matter of practice (see Chapter 4).

8. **Learn Effective Communication Skills.**
   Being a good listener, knowing how to ask questions nonthreateningly, and understanding human nature will all contribute to your sales success. Take advantage of any opportunity to learn more about the fascinating field of communication.

9. **Achieve the Ability to Manage Several Customers.**
   You cannot be successful if you only have one customer. Managing a network of prospects and customers is an art as well as a science—you want them to feel that they have your undivided attention. The meticulous account records you keep will assist you with this.

10. **Strategize to Integrate Experiences, Observations, and Study into Your Plan for Success.**
    When you are in sales, you need all your faculties working for you. As you deal with many customers, you will learn a lot about human nature and about the businesses they are in. Keep your eyes open for ideas and tips that can make you even more successful. Review the people you know in your personal life to see if you can get leads or references there. Scan the newspaper for names of businesspeople who have been promoted and congratulate them. Don't overlook anything in your quest for success.

SELLING YOURSELF FIRST

"People buy from people."

You may have heard this expression before. It is an important truth worth remembering. Consider your own purchases. How often have you purchased something from someone you didn't like? Bank customers are no different; like everyone else, they prefer to do business with individuals they like and trust. Remember: that businessperson, realtor, or professional is looking for a *banker*, not a bank.

One of the surest ways to sell yourself first is to *show an interest in your customer.* We all like to be noticed and listened to. Customers want to feel like special people, just like the rest of us. If you can demonstrate to your customer that you are genuinely interested in him and care about his needs, you will have achieved that critical state called "rapport" before you've mentioned your services in any detail. As Mary Kay Ash, founder of Mary Kay Cosmetics, says; "Every person has an invisible sign on their chest that says, 'Make me feel important.'"

Other things that help you sell yourself include:

- Visible confidence, both in yourself and your product.
- A friendly demeanor.
- Appropriate dress and personal appearance.
- An eagerness to listen.
- A demonstrated desire to help your customer.

PACKAGE YOURSELF AS A WINNER

When you go in to see your prospect, you are competing with many different people for his time—other salespeople, coworkers, business associates—and you want to make sure that your appearance helps you earn the right to do business with his company.

People often do judge books by their covers, and they certainly judge people by their appearance, especially when they that person is there to sell. So your ability to distinguish yourself and package yourself as a winner will be your first advantage in getting business. Following is a five-step strategy for packaging yourself as a winner.

Look the Part Did you know that people form their first impression of you in seven seconds? In only seven seconds you create a lasting impression on your audience. Because this impression is formed so rapidly, you have only your appearance, facial expression, and carriage to communicate a positive message. Your education, competence, and experience are not yet in evidence.

Being appropriately dressed is the simplest way to set yourself apart and show in a dignified, yet unmistakable way that you are a winner.

Choose only the finest fabrics in classic lines. You'll find that by spending more for quality garments, you'll actually save money by being able to wear them longer. Think in terms of *cost per wearing*. And be adamant about alterations. Your garments must fit perfectly in order to convey a sense of elegance and personal power.

By dressing appropriately, you can "stack the deck" in your favor. Psychologists tell us about the Halo Effect, which says that if you are perceived positively in your first meeting with someone, that person will come to expect all things from you to be good, thus endowing you with a halo of positiveness.

So if your prospect gets a good first impression, she will prejudge your work, expecting it to be of excellent quality. This Halo Effect can be a powerful ally for you, making your path to success a little smoother—all by merely dressing in a way that says, "I can do it, and I can do it well."

Show Enthusiasm

Winners are enthusiastic people; they exude positive energy that attracts others to them.

You can simulate energy by moving decisively at a purposeful pace, with good posture and a straight back.

You want to give the impression that your energy is just barely in check.

The foundation of enthusiasm is found in good health habits: proper diet, exercise, and adequate sleep. You can't *do* good if you don't *feel* good. Aside from the obvious benefits of physical fitness, there is an interesting phenomenon that crops up in study after study: thinness is associated with executive success. Lean people are seen as being more in control of circumstances and events, and they have a better chance of getting ahead.

One way to protect your enthusiasm is to associate with positive people. Winners surround themselves with winning people, winning ideas, winning projects, winning literature, winning situations. Negativism can sap your energy and drain your creativity.

In every organization, there is a group of people who are always negative—they see the worst in everything the company does. And they can't wait to let everyone know. (Misery loves company.) You must refuse to lend any of your time to these doomsayers. Anything that doesn't energize or add to your obviously detracts from you.

Another strategy for keeping your enthusiasm high is to free yourself from worry about thing you can't control. It's easy to fall into the trap of worrying about everything. But if you spend your time worrying about things outside your control, you will have no energy left over for your job and your personal relationships.

There's only one thing that you have total control over in your workplace: your attitude. You have a choice each day to create the kind of day you want to have. Customers will take their cues from your attitude and will instinctively respond more favorably to you if you are

positive. Attitude is contagious; is yours worth catching?

Deliver a Consistent Image

Your image accrues over time. Your prospects and customers will believe what they see about you, and if the message is consistently positive, they will form an excellent impression of you and your capabilities.

You can use your appearance to reinforce the image you want your customers to have of you by being consistent. If you are always well-groomed and professionally attired, people will believe that you are competent.

Your image should never be an accident, but a carefully orchestrated statement of who you are and who you are not. Remember: It's the inconsistencies that people remember—the one day you "dressed down" or the argument you had in a meeting. They will tend to magnify these negative moments and forget all the positive impressions, so consistency of image is very important.

Develop a Sense of Humor

A sense of humor is almost a required characteristic for success, because the challenges of a selling career can be overwhelming at times. The best closers in the business have a 50 percent close rate, so we know that some failure is part of the job. If you take it all *too* seriously, you run the risk of burning out early on.

A sense of humor can help you offset the stress that so often accompanies career success. It identifies you as someone who can "roll with the punches" and who has a sense of balance about life. And your customers will appreciate that when they have tough issues to discuss with you.

A touch of humor can soften a mistake, disarm an enemy, or save an unpleasant moment. Humor builds rapport; laughter clears the air. A sense of humor is associated with charm, and being charming is a positive quality for smooth relationships with your customers and coworkers.

Be Dependable

Once you have created a favorable impression, the next step is to build credibility, or cause your customer to trust you.

Consider how often you have had a business relationship with someone you did not trust. How do you feel when you believe you are being cheated in some way? That sick sensation in the pit of your stomach when you think someone is not being honest with you is the same feeling your customer gets if he or she feels you cannot be trusted.

Building trust is a key factor in successful selling. To do that:

Never say anything to a customer that you do not believe to be true or promise anything that you cannot possibly carry out.

If you demonstrate repeatedly that your customer can count on your word, credibility will grow on its own. This includes not making vague statements about your capabilities or your bank's services in order to color the truth and make a sale. Those statements have a way of coming back to you in very unpleasant forms!

Credibility also means thorough follow-up in providing information to your customer. It means:

- Being on time for your scheduled meetings.
- Returning phone calls on the day received.
- Making sure your customer knows other key people in the bank.
- Keeping your customer informed of any changes that may affect his or her business with you.

All these "little things" add up to the biggest asset a salesperson can have:

Credibility

If you achieve credibility, you will have earned something that cannot be bought at any price.

WHERE TO GET HELP

Professional Sales Organizations

Bank Marketing Association
309 W. Washington St.
Chicago, IL 60606
Publication: *Bank Marketing*
Fin'l Inst. Marketing Association
111 E. Wacker Dr.
Chicago, IL 60601
Publication: *Marketing News*
Bank membership
Regional Meetings

Individual membership
American Marketing Association
250 S. Wacker Dr.
Chicago, IL 60606
Publication: *Marketing News*
Monthly meetings in major cities
Individual and corporate membership

National Association for Professional Saleswomen
P.O. Box 255708

Sacramento, CA 95865
(916) 484-1234
Publication: *Successful Saleswomen*
Monthly meetings in major cities
Individual membership

Sales Publications

Sales & Marketing Management
Subscription Services Department
P.O. Box 588
King of Prussia, PA 19506

Success!
P.O. Box 3036
Harlan, IA 51593-2097
800-247-5470

Bank Marketing
309 W. Washington St.
Chicago, IL 60606
(302) 782-1442

Bottomline
National Council of Savings Institutions
1101 15th St. N.W.
Washington, DC 20005-5070
(some sales articles)

For help in improving presentation skills:

Toastmasters International
2200 N. Grand Ave.
Santa Ana, CA 92711
Chapters in most cities

WORKSHEET: THE SALES PROCESS

1. How do you feel about being a salesperson?
   - ☐ Excited
   - ☐ Anxious
   - ☐ Ready to prove myself
   - ☐ Reluctant
   - ☐ Enthusiastic
   - ☐ Embarrassed
   - ☐ Eager
   - ☐ Overwhelmed

   Now discuss these feelings with one other person in the bank you feel close to. Being aware of how much you are looking forward to or are dreading selling it is the first step toward creating your success.

2. Write three good open questions you could use with your prospects. Write a prospect's name next to each question, and resolve to ask it.

   1. _____

   2. _____

   3. _____

3. In reading through "Selling Yourself First," you may have been thinking about what you could do to enhance your image. Take a moment to write down some changes you'd like to make in your image.

   1.

   2.

   3.

   4.

   5.

2 Prospecting Techniques

What's behind that door I cannot tell,
But this I know, and I know it well:
The more doors I open, The more I sell.

Prospecting is the process of collecting names of potential customers. We'll look at four ways to collect prospects:

1. From referrals.
2. From published information.
3. From telemarketing.
4. From direct-mail campaigns.

PROSPECTING FROM REFERRALS

The easiest way to get the name of a prospective customer is through a referral: a potential customer's name give to you by someone you know.

How do you get referrals? You ask for them. Whom do you ask? Anyone who might be able to help. This includes your current customers, professional-association colleagues, friends, neighbors—virtually anyone you meet who could be helpful.

If you are hesitant about asking for a referral, consider this: Most people are flattered to be asked for their opinion. You'll probably be surprised at how helpful your customers can be to your sales efforts if you'll just let them. And it certainly is a benefit to call Mr. Big and be able to say, "Jane at XYZ Manufacturing suggested I give you a call."

Asking for a referral does not have to be a torturous process. It's as simple as saying to a pension plan customer, "Jane, which of your colleagues might be interested in a similar pension plan?" If you truly believe in your bank and your products, then be confident about finding out who else may benefit from them.

If you do your prospecting right, customers will begin to come to you with names before you've even asked!

Professional Leads

Realtors, attorneys, accountants, and financial planners are excellent sources for prospects. They can provide you with prospects who are ready to do business with you. You should be calling on these people and developing good relationships with them.

A professional lead can result in a "win-win-win" situation. The realtor or accountant gets the added prestige of "knowing someone at the bank"; the prospect gets the status, security, and convenience of being a "preferred" customer and you win by getting a new customer.

Remember: Anyone who provides you with a referral deserves your thanks, whether you turn the prospect into a customer or not. A note is usually sufficient, but you may want to consider a flower arrangement or some other gift, depending on how large a customer the prospect turns out to be.

Existing Customers

An existing customer who does not yet have a particular product is an excellent prospect for that product. A relationship already exists between you and the customer. The customer already has confidence and trust in you. The customer gets the added convenience of single-stop banking. The customer also feels increased status because of your interest and attention.

PROSPECTING FROM PUBLISHED INFORMATION

There are several published sources of prospects for you to tap into. These include:

Newspapers — Learn to scale the daily newspaper for leads. These come in the form of new business openings, promotions, marriage and birth announcements, feature articles about local businesses, want ads, announcements of Chamber of Commerce seminars, etc. You can turn all of this information into a prospect list that you can use to set up sales calls.

Business & Professional Organization Membership Lists — Many organizations will provide you with a copy of their membership list when you become a member or if you make a presentation to their membership. Some organizations will provide you with their membership list for a nominal fee. The membership list can be an excellent source of prospects. Examples include trade organizations, service organizations, the Chamber of Commerce, and professional societies.

Manufacturers' Directories — These publications list manufacturers by state, county, city, and SIC code. They can be found in your library or ordered from the local Chamber of Commerce.

Business Periodicals — These include publications like *New England Business, Forbes, Fortune, Business Week, Barron's,* and the local *Business Digest*.

Dun & Bradstreet Half-Million and Million Dollar Directories — These publications, found in your library, list all of the firms that gross over $500,000 and over $1,000,000 annually in sales. They give the address and telephone number of the company and the officers' names.

These sources give you the most valuable information you need to prospect: a name. It is much easier to get an appointment with a potential customer if you know whom to ask for.

Telephone Book — By merely looking through the yellow pages under "Accountants," "Attorneys," "Physicians," etc., you can develop a prospect list.

PROSPECTING WITH THE TELEPHONE

The telephone can be your best friend in prospecting. It can help you contact a great many people in a short amount of time, and it can save you time by helping you qualify a prospect before you make a sales call. In short, it saves you time and makes you more effective.

The key to effective use of the telephone in prospecting is to have a system. This means planning whom you are going to call, using a telephone log to record all the phone calls you make, and following up promptly. Try this system:

1. Set aside a specific time each week for prospecting phone calls. Experiment to find out what times are best. Monday mornings and Friday afternoons are usually not the best times to reach people. You may find that you need to call at 8:00 A.M., rather than 9:00, to reach people before they go into meetings. Sometimes 5:00 P.M. is the best time to reach a busy executive. Never call a customer at home in the evening. This is an invasion of privacy and shows a lack of professionalism on your part.

2. Make a list of the phone calls you plan to make. Include contact name, title, company name and address, and phone number. Planning your work makes you more effective.

3. Keep a dated record of each call you make. This helps you remember whom you called when, and it helps you plan your follow-up strategy. It also helps you to trace the development of your relationship with the customer. Remember to take notes during the call so you won't have to rely on your memory for important facts.

4. Design a standard follow-up procedure and stick to it. For example, after you've made the fifteen prospecting phone calls for the day, give your secretary the names and addresses and have a form letter sent. It might say:

> Thank you for your time today. I've enclosed a brochure on _____ for your review. If you want to take advantage of this service, please sign here and mail to me at the following address: _____. We appreciate your interest in Community Bank.

Success in telephoning requires a system. Design a system that works for you and stick to it, week after week. It's a numbers game: The more calls you make the more successful you will be. (You'll learn more about telephone selling in Chapter 9.)

PROSPECTING WITH DIRECT MAIL

Direct mail is a sales strategy that can also be used for prospecting. A direct-mail campaign is a mailing to a selected set of individuals to generate new business. Occasions for a direct-mail campaign include:

- Announcement of a new product or service.
- Announcement of a new employee at the bank.
- A re-emphasis on an existing product or service.
- A significant date in the bank's history.
- A special event.

Direct-mail campaigns can be conducted around any event that you deem will be effective in obtaining new customers or in selling new services to established customers.

The bank can establish a formal direct-mail campaign, or you can start one of your own to supplement your prospecting strategy.

You may want to begin by writing to all current customers to thank them for their continued patronage and tell them about additional services they could be benefiting from. This gives you a chance to make that "sales call" through the mail, which is especially effective with those customers who don't come into the bank often. A letter to prospective customers about the advantages of your bank can stimulate new interest.

Be sure to send out only as many letters per week as you can follow up on. A letter without a follow-up is a waste of paper and postage.

Follow up on your letters over the telephone. Begin by asking if the person received your letter, and then inquire whether there are any questions you can answer. Find out if the person is interested in the ser-

vice, and if so, offer to fill out the paperwork and drop it in the mail. Make it easy for the customer to do business with you. Use this contact to spark their interest in taking a look at your bank.

Why not make it part of your personal commitment to selling to send out fifteen letters per week and follow up on them on Friday morning? You can increase the effectiveness of your direct-mail campaign by keeping statistics on such things as which follow-up day of the week provided you with the most contacts; for each mailing, how many sales you made; what geographic areas seemed to produce the most sales; which products generated the most interest; and which market segments responded most often.

The easiest way to start a direct-mail campaign is to design a form letter and merge it with the prospect names and addresses. With a word-processing system, each customer receives a personalized letter, even though the original letter was only typed once. Occasionally you may want to add a handwritten note across the bottom of the letter for some personal remark to a customer you know, such as: "Jane, you mentioned that you were interested in this the last time we talked."

Your letters should always focus on the benefits to the customer of doing business with your bank. Put yourself in the customer's shoes and ask, "What's in it for me?" If you letter doesn't address the benefits of the recommended service, it will probable fall on deaf ears and be a waste of time.

Be sure to include in your closing remarks that you will be following up soon. Don't leave the customer hanging about what happens next. A simple statement like "I'll be calling next week to discuss your interest in taking advantage of this new option" lets the customer know what to expect. Then, when you do call, the person will be expecting your call.

It's very important to address letters to a specific person. Most of us don't even open mail that is addressed to "Occupant," "Current Resident," or "Treasurer" because we already have a clue that it's an advertisement of some kind. *If you can't get a name, don't send the letter.* With commercial customers, call the office and ask who is in charge of cash management or who the owner is. If you identify yourself and ask politely, people usually will give you this information.

Successful salespeople prospect continually, keeping a steady stream of new business opportunities coming their way. A consistent prospecting system will help you avoid slumps and always keep you poised for the future. You can use all four of these methods—asking for referrals, using public lists, doing telemarketing, and sending regular mailings—to ensure your success in business development.

WORKSHEET: PROSPECTING TECHNIQUES

1. Write an opening statement for telephone prospecting. Include in it *who* you are, *where* you are from, *what* you want to discuss, and how much *time* you will need. Remember to include the *benefits* to the prospect of granting you the time on the phone and then an appointment.

2. Write down the names of five businesspeople you know who do not bank with you now.

   1.

   2.

   3.

   4.

   5.

3. Write down the names of five customers who could be doing more business with you.

   1.

   2.

   3.

   4.

   5.

Call all ten people *today*!
Repeat this exercise every three weeks.

3 The Sales Call

The average sale is made on the fifth try. Unless you are asking five times, you are not trying hard enough.

People don't fail; they just give up trying.

According to a recent survey 75 percent of all business executives say you cannot get in to see them without an appointment. Although "dropping in" may occasionally be appropriate, it is usually frowned upon in business. You immediately establish yourself as a professional when you phone ahead for an appointment.

HOW TO GET AN APPOINTMENT OVER THE PHONE

1. Pick a quiet place.
2. Use a script (opening statement prepared in Chapter 2).
3. Take ten deep breaths.
4. Stand up.
5. Smile! It shows in your voice.
6. Be friendly, not authoritative.
7. State your name clearly.
8. Say, "Thank-you for your time."
9. State benefits clearly.
10. Listen and take notes.
11. Get a commitment.
12. Summarize.
13. Say "Thank-you. I'll see you at _____ on _____."

Smile when you confirm the appointment over the phone. It changes the tone of your voice!

PRE-CALL PLANNING

The activities you go through before a sales call, whether it's your first call on a prospect or a repeat call, are critical to your success during the call. There are four steps in pre-call planning:

1. Determine an objective.
2. Gather account information.
3. Review the call.
4. Prepare yourself psychologically.

Determine an Objective

Every sales call should have a business objective. A professional salesperson never "drops in for no special reason." Every action the banker takes should be planned and should contribute to a sale.

Before you make a sales call, either over the telephone or in person, decide on an objective. Ask yourself, "What do I want to accomplish?" The answer to that question is your *objective*. Possible objectives include:

- To sell a service.
- To schedule an appointment.
- To qualify the customer for your product or service.
- To determine the customer's financial objectives.
- To discover who can make a decision.

If it is your first call on an account, your objective may be simply to introduce yourself to a key person.

Whatever your objective is, make sure you have one before investing your time. The sales cycle discussed in Chapter 1 is an excellent model for determining a series of objectives for the selling process. A sale is usually made up of several objectives that have been accomplished one by one.

In planning a call, try to look at your long-term objective and determine what is needed in the short run to help you get there.

Gather Account Information

Once you have determined your objective, the next step is to learn as much as you can about the customer and her business.

Analyze her situation by asking questions like, "Who...," "What...," "How..." about the business. Good sources of information include customer files, business periodicals, and other bank personnel. This step not only provides you with clues about how to approach the account, but gives you something to talk about in the first few minutes of the call. Be sure to find out what business she is doing with your bank now. It could be very embarrassing to suggest a service, only to find out that your "prospect" has been a customer for years!

Review the Call

Mentally rehearse the call. Think about the objections the prospect might raise and how you will answer them. Then the call itself won't be a trial run but a smooth performance. Try to eliminate surprises by being prepared.

Prepare Yourself Psychologically

Your attitude and level of enthusiasm in the first ten seconds of the call say more about you than anything that follows. Therefore, it is important for you to prepare yourself psychologically to present a positive attitude.

Do whatever it takes for you to feel at your best before the call. If you know that jogging in the morning enthuses you, do it before an important call. If you know you need time alone to think before a call, make sure you schedule that time into your day. The face you want to present to your customer is your best face.

Thinking about the value of your products to the customer will get you focused on satisfying his objectives.

OTHER ELEMENTS OF PRE-CALL PLANNING

1. Schedule an appointment. This ensures that the prospect is ready and waiting for you. Be sure to let him know how much time you'd like.

2. Send a confirmation letter. This informs the customer of the date, time, reason for the call, and general subject for discussion. This reinforces your professionalism and distinguishes you from all the other people calling on that businessperson.

3. Inform others. This ensures you that they will be available for the help you may need. Send them a copy of the confirmation letter. By lining up your support team, you won't be left hanging.

4. Hold a brief strategy meeting if there are several people from your bank involved. Make sure they have all the facts and understand the role you'd like them to play.

5. Prepare your presentation materials. Make sure you have a business card, sales kit, brochure, visuals, calculator, etc. You want to have everything you need at your fingertips.

6. Call the customer the day before. This reconfirms the appointment and accommodates any changes in his schedule.

The better you prepare *before* the call, the better your performance will be *during* the call. It's difficult to convince a customer you're interested in his business if you are not prepared. The key is to be so prepared that when you are face-to-face with your customer, you can focus all your energy on building a relationship, not on worrying about what to do next or where your pen is.

MAKING THE CALL

The sales call is your opportunity to sell yourself, sell your bank, and create an interest in your products. It's also your opportunity to learn a lot about your prospect's business. (See Table 3.1 for an outline of the stages of a sales call.)

SELLING YOURSELF

A first impression is almost impossible to erase, so make sure that you appear professional and well-groomed. This includes appropriate dress, hairstyle, cosmetics, and fragrance. The general rule is to be conservative. You don't want someone to remember you as "the one with the kinky hairdo" or "the purple plaid suit with the yellow tie." A sales call is not the place to make a fashion statement.

Being on time will add to your professional image. It shows that you respect the customer's schedule and that you are well-organized. If it's unavoidable that you will be late, have the courtesy to call and give your customer the opportunity to reschedule.

Arriving a few minutes early is a good strategy because it gives you time to meet your customer's secretary and to observe details about the business. A casual conversation with a receptionist or secretary may pro-

vide you with valuable information. Concentrate on merely collecting information, however; do not make judgments about the account. It is too early to accept impressions as reality. Use these few minutes to listen, observe, and review your call strategy.

When you meet your customer for the first time, offer your hand and state your name, title, and company clearly. Then offer your business card and ask for the customer's ("I'd like you to have one of my cards. May I have one of yours?"). This gives you a moment to relax and also ensures that in future correspondence, you will always spell her name correctly and use her correct title. Nothing makes a worse impression than to send someone a letter with her name spelled wrong!

OPENING THE CONVERSATION

As you begin the call, state why you are there and the general area you wish to discuss. Even if you already

TABLE 3.1 The Sales Call Stages.

Opening

Introduce yourself.
State purpose of visit.
Indicate time you will spend.
Discuss general area of interest.
Listen for sales opportunities.
Gain rapport.

Body

Deliver an initial benefits statement.
Use open and reflective questions to define needs.
Listen for sales opportunities.
Use reference selling.
Talk about your products in terms of benefits, advantages, and exclusive features.
Summarize key points of interest.
Create a desire for your products.

Close

Summarize points discussed.
Emphasize points of agreement.
Gain commitment on some point.
Agree on an action plan.

Follow Up

Confirm your agreement in writing.
Call or visit periodically to check satisfaction.
Stay abreast of business changes (sales opportunities).

---

conveyed this on the telephone, restate it in case your customer forgot. Spend a few minutes explaining your role with the bank. Tell your customer why you are there, and make it worth his or her time to see you.

If you appear relaxed and cheerful, your customer is more likely to be receptive to you. If it takes practice for you to be relaxed on a sales call, try acting it out with a colleague ahead of time.

One way to overcome the sales-call jitters is to have a sales kit. A sales kit should contain only those items of interest to the customer you are calling on. You should be thoroughly familiar with the contents and feel com-

fortable using the aid. The most effective sales kit is one prepared by you. A broad overview of the services of your bank and the benefits of your products would be appropriate for the first call. (You can read more about sales kits in Chapter 4.)

Use open and reflective questions to draw your customer out and get him talking. Remember that a successful sales call is one in which the businessperson talks 80 percent of the time and the banker talks only 20 percent of the time. Be alert for clues that suggest a problem you can solve or a load you can lighten.

Never spend more time with a customer than you were scheduled for unless the customer explicity offers to spend more time with you. It is appropriate to say something like, "It's 1:30, and I had asked to spend only this half hour with you. Would you like to stop now or continue?" If your customer indicates that he would like to spend more time, then he has given you the OK to extend your appointment. If he says he'd rather stick to the schedule, wrap it up and leave. The point is to be sensitive to the customer's schedule and to remember that you are a visitor in his office.

CALL FOLLOW-UP

Call follow-up is the element that distinguishes the professional salesperson from the unschooled. This includes:

- A letter thanking your customer for his interest in your bank. This letter should include a summary of your meeting and what you are going to do next. (A sample letter follows in Figure 3.1).
- A phone call with the information the customer requested.
- A briefing about the customer to any other people in your bank you may need help from or who can profit from the information.
- Documentation of the call in the customer's file.

Call follow-up is important after every sales call, not just the first one. It is another reminder of you and the bank to the customer.

To be effective, your call follow-up must be timely. A thank-you letter received three weeks after the call is meaningless and clearly shows the customer that he or she is not high on your priority list.

HOW TO MAKE A SALES CALL

1. Find a "live" prospect.
2. Research the prospect's business.
3. Call the prospect and give him/her a reason for seeing you.
4. Prepare for the call. Review facts about the business, gather sales aids, get directions to the office, and then relax.

Figure 3.1 Sample Sales Call Follow-Up Letter.

Mr. James Jones, Vice President
Amalgamated Products
2 Amalgamated Way
Pleasantville, TX 75024

Dear Jim,

It was a pleasure meeting with you this morning to discuss your cash management requirements. I enjoyed learning more about your business and touring the plant. With your busy schedule, it certainly makes sense to consider some new ways to handle your cash flow.

Jim, I am convinced that our cash management system would save you valuable time and give you a better return on your money. By getting started next month, you would see the benefits immediately in terms of less paperwork and more flexibility. I think you'll agree that your time is too valuable to spend on routine transactions.

I will call you Thursday to discuss an implementation plan. Thanks again for your interest in our bank. I'm looking forward to working with you.

Very truly yours,

Susan A. Smith
Vice President

5. Arrive at the prospect's office a few minutes early. Use this time to talk with the secretary. Look, listen, and observe. Focus on collecting information, not on evaluating it.
6. Greet the prospect with a firm handshake, a smile, and a pleasant comment. Offer your business card and ask for the prospect's card.
7. Give a one-sentence statement about why you are there and the time you plan to spend. Recheck that the prospect has this amount of time to spend before you get started. Summarize for him/her what you plan to cover.
8. Ask if there are other points the prospect would like you to cover.
9. Begin by finding out more about the prospect's needs and interests. A simple way to begin this conversation is to say, "I know that in your business, such-and-such is always a concern. How do you manage this at XYZ?" Take notes.
10. After an appropriate interval, give an overview of the services and benefits you offer, tailoring it to the business your prospect is in. Use reference selling to explain how others have profited from your products and services. This is the time for enthusiasm and pride. Make the prospect want to know more.
11. Respond to questions and handle objections promptly. Do this in a calm, professional, and friendly manner. Remember: You are a visitor in your prospect's office and not there by right.
12. Wrap up your discussion by re-emphasizing the benefits.
13. Ask your prospect for a commitment on some point.
14. State what you have agreed upon and what each of you will do next.
15. Thank the prospect for his or her time.
16. Follow up promptly with a letter.

WORKSHEET: THE SALES CALL

1. Make an appointment to call on one of your prospects.
   Who is it?
   Date and time of appointment:

2. What is your objective?

3. What objections do you anticipate?

4. How will you present your products?

5. Background information on prospect:

4 Effective Sales Presentations

He who has a thing to sell
And goes and whispers in a well,
Is not so apt to get the dollars
As he who climbs a tree and hollers.

A presentation is your opportunity to present yourself and your products in the most favorable light to the customer. A good presentation can make the sale; a poor one can guarantee that you won't get the sale. Therefore, it is important to spend time working on your presentation skills.

The great advantage of a presentation over a written report is that the presentation allows you to cut through the barriers of misperception, differing values, and other psychological interferences because you are right there, interacting with the prospect. A presentation gives you the opportunity to directly address the needs and concerns of the customer and move your business case toward the close.

SELLING BENEFITS — THE KEY

Whether you are selling a commercial checking account to a small business or trying to convince a car dealership to offer financing through your bank, you have to demonstrate the value to them of accepting your recommendation. People don't buy products or ideas until they have seen their value. Your job as a salesperson is to help them see that the value you offer far outweighs the price. Remember: No one likes to be sold, but everyone likes to buy!

Value is conveyed in terms of benefits. A presentation should be designed to highlight the benefits to the customer of building a relationship with you.

The key technique is to highlight those benefits your customer is interested in — those that will help him achieve his objectives. It is critical that you spend time upfront understanding your customer's objectives before you give a sales presentation. Otherwise, your "canned pitch" will be lost on the customer. A canned pitch is a speech, a one-way process of communication. An effective presentation is an interactive, two-way discussion with your customer.

DEVELOPING A PRESENTATION SYSTEM

The sale of any banking service lends itself well to a four-point presentation system in which you stress the customer's concerns, the strengths of your bank in meeting those concerns, the package of services you are recommending, and the relationship you and your customer will enjoy. This four-point system is really just four ideas, in a logical order, that can be used in a formal presentation with flip charts; in an informal presentation to two or three people across a desk, using a desktop easel; or verbally, one-on-one with the decision-maker.

The beauty of the system is that once you have it in your mind, you can use it for any sales situation that arises, merely customizing it for your prospect. By having the key ideas firmly planted in your mind, you're free to concentrate on the prospect, observing her reactions and answering her questions.

I have seen this system used successfully by bankers across the country, in all types of selling situations. The format is on the following pages, followed by a sample script and sample flip charts.

Visual aids are important in selling. They allow you to guide your customer through a scenario, helping him visualize success and prosperity. People retain a great deal more of what you say when your presentation is accompanied by visual aids. Later in this chapter you will learn how to prepare different visual aids, with the pros and cons of each type.

KEY IDEAS

A SUCCESSFUL SYSTEM FOR A STRONG PRESENTATION FOR COMMERCIAL CUSTOMERS

Key Idea #1: The customer's needs, stated as benefits.

A. Improved profit
B. Streamlined operations
C. Employee retention
D. Time savings

Transitional Phrase: "If I can show you how we can help you meet your objectives, would you begin banking with us today?"

Key Idea #2: The strengths and capabilities of your bank. (Give a personalized example of how each affects the customer.)

A. Community-oriented.
  — Investment in community.
  — Participation in local events.

B. Solid experience with local businesses.
  — Experts in each area.
  — Over 100 years of quality financial advice.

C. Full service.
  — Variety of services gives you flexibility.
  — "We will be there as you grow."

D. The personal touch.
  — You deal with decision-makers.
  — "We work for you."

Transitional Phrase: "Mr./(Ms.) Prospect, wouldn't you agree that this is the kind of bank you'd like to do business with?"

Key Idea #3: The tailored product package. Keep it simple. Group products in natural categories, such as day-to-day transactions, investments, retirement planning. Or short-term and long term. Or by benefits as expressed in No. 1 above. Use a picture if it helps.

A. Day-to-day banking	A. Phase 1	A. Improved profit
B. Investments OR	B. Phase 2 OR	B. Streamlined operations
C. Retirement planning	C. Phase 3	C. Time savings

Transitional Phrase: "Mr./(Ms.) Prospect, wouldn't you agree that this banking system would help you achieve your objectives?"

Key Idea #4: The successful relationship you and the prospect can look forward to.

Pictures and graphics work well here. You can use a handshake, your bank's logo, a staircase to success, a sales chart — whatever would be meaningful for your customer. Leave this page in view if a question session follows.

Closing Statement: "Why don't we get started today?"

KEY IDEAS

SAMPLE SCRIPT FOR A COMMERCIAL CUSTOMER

Key Idea #1

- Improved profit
- Streamlined operations
- Employee retention
- Time savings

"Mr. Prospect, the last time we talked, you mentioned that your major concerns in cash management were to increase profits, making your money work harder for you; to remove the tedious work from your bookkeeping department; to hold onto good employees; and to save time in the operation of your business.

"If I can show you how Great Bank can help you achieve those objectives, would you begin banking with me today?"

Key Idea #2

- Community-oriented

"Let me tell you a little about the bank you would be dealing with. We've been a strong financial leader in this community for over 100 years. The money your neighbors and business associates invest with us stays right here in our community, making this a better place to live. I'm sure you know that we were involved in the reconstruction of the railroad depot and helped fund the senior-citizen housing."

- Solid experience

"We have a lot of accumulated expertise about business, having worked with the businesspeople in this community through many situations. We can not only provide you with the services you need, but also offer an experienced perspective."

- Full service

"We offer everything you need to maintain your current operations and much more to help you grow. We can take care of your personal financial needs and those of your employees."

- Personal touch

"We pride ourselves on the personal touch. You will only need one contact at the bank — me — to handle all of your affairs.

Ms. Prospect, isn't this the kind of bank *you'd* like to be doing business with?"

Key Idea #3

- Day-to-day banking

"Here's how our relationship would work. For your day-to-day transactions, you could profit from our sweep account, which maximizes the return on your funds. Convenience services such as payroll accounting, night deposit,

	and 24-hour banking will save you a lot of time."
• Investments	"We'll work with you to develop an investment strategy that will offer growth with security and keep your balance sheet strong. A combination of CDs, mutual funds, and an insurance program will accomplish your objectives."
• Retirement planning	"Although it's a long way off, you are in an excellent position to begin planning for retirement with a pension plan. You will get immediate tax advantages, and over the long term, not only will you be providing amply for yourself and your family, but you will be offering a benefit that's important for attracting and retaining good employees."
	"Mr. Prospect, wouldn't you agree that this financial plan will help you achieve your objectives?"

Key Idea #4

"Ms. Prospect, our relationship will be a partnership, one in which we can help you prosper and grow."

"Why don't we get started today by setting up the payroll system? I can work with your bookkeeper to

insure the smooth transition of all your affairs. All you'll see is an improved cash flow and fewer worries.

"Ms. Prospect, I'm looking forward to being a part of your team."

SAMPLE PRESENTATION FLIP CHARTS FOR BUSINESS OWNERS

- Improved profit.
- Streamlined operations.
- Employee retention.
- Time savings.

- Community-oriented.
- Strong expertise.
- Full service.
- The personal touch.

- Day-to-day banking.
- Investments.
- Retirement planning.

Great Bank
and
YOU
A growing partnership.

KEY IDEAS

THE FOUR-POINT SYSTEM FOR REALTORS

Key Idea #1:
The customer's needs, stated as benefits.

A. More successful closings.
B. Streamlined process.
C. Open line of communication.
D. Time savings.

Transitional Phrases: "Are there any other needs you would like me to add?" "If I can show you how we can help you meet your objectives, would you begin sending your clients to us?"

Key Idea #2: The strength and capabilities of your company. (Give a personalized example of how each affects the customer.)

A. Experienced originators.
   — Participate in hundreds of deals each year.
   — Seasoned professionals.

B. Flexible programs.
   — Geared to your clients.
   — A program for every budget.

C. Full-service banking.
   — Can help clients with total financial planning.
   — We understand the environment.

D. No. 1 lender in the market.
   — You deal with decision-makers.
   — We work for you.

Transitional phrase: "Mr./(Ms.) Realtor, wouldn't you agree that this is the kind of company *you'd* like to do business with?"

Key Idea #3:
The tailored offering.
Keep it simple. Group products in natural categories or focus on the process.

A. Application process
B. Closing
C. Servicing

OR

A. Product Group 1
B. Product Group 2
C. Product Group 3

Transitional phrase: "Mr./(Ms.) Realtor, wouldn't you agree this system would help you achieve your objectives?"

Key Idea #4: The successful relationship you and the realtor can look forward to.

Pictures and graphics work well here. You can use a handshake, a sales chart, a money tree — whatever will be most meaningful for your customers. Leave this page in view if a question session follows.

Closing Statement
"What deals are you working on that I can help you close?"

SAMPLE PRESENTATION FLIP CHART FOR REALTORS

Benefits
- Time savings
- Improved productivity
- Open line of communication
- PROFIT

Your Organization
- Stability
- Market presence
- Flexibility
- Responsiveness

The Package
- 72 hour verbal commitment
  2 1/2 week written commitment
- Training of salespeople
- Direct communication with loan officer
- More closings/More commissions

The Relationship

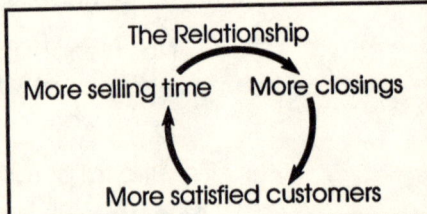

DELIVERY OF THE PRESENTATION

A presentation is a sharing of ideas. You have to practice a presentation until your words become ideas. Memorizing your presentation can be fatal; — if you forget one word, you're lost. A more effective technique is to design visuals that help you find your way and then practice several times with the visuals. For the four-point system, sample flip charts are on pages 62 and 64.

Begin your presentation with an interest-grabbing statement. Try to involve the audience early on by directing your comments to their specific areas of interest.

Questions from the audience should be answered as they are raised. To solicit questions, ask, "What are your questions?" rather than "Do you have any questions?"

When you ask a question, deliver it to a specific person. "Joe, how would you be able to use the additional funds provided by this service?" will elicit more information than "Do any of you see the benefit to this service?" which might get you a blank stare.

The following list gives a few guidelines for handling questions:

1. Wait. Allow people to ask. There's always a question.
2. Repeat the question before answering it if your audience is large.
3. Keep your answers brief and to the point.
4. Direct your answer to everyone, not just to the questioner.
5. Maintain eye contact when answering a question.
6. Use visuals to make the answer clear.
7. Don't talk down to or argue with the questioner.
8. When you don't know an answer, say so and offer to find it.
9. When you don't understand the question, ask for an example.
10. Follow the question period with a strong closing statement.

A brief note about jokes: Don't use them. Humor is an individual thing, and not everybody thinks the same things are funny. Ineffective use of humor can ruin an otherwise impressive presentation.

Sexist language is another trap. If you fall into it, you may offend someone in the audience and lose your message. Remember: Not everyone vocalizes that they are offended.

Close your presentation with a strong statement that is tied to your opening statement. This is the one thought you want to leave your audience with.

TEAM PRESENTATIONS

Team presentations can be very effective if carried out properly. They keep the interest of the audience by exposing them to different voice tones, appearances, and presentation styles. It is also a good way to use experts for providing information on some topic of interest to the audience.

The key to an effective team presentation is to realize that it is still only one presentation. Introductions of presentors should occur before the presentation, with no breaks for introductions between presentors.

Each presenter should finish with a strong closing statement that leads into the next presenter's opening statement. Do not use "Thank-you" as a closing statement. It is off the point and robs you of the opportunity for a strong close.

As soon as a presenter turns to leave, the next presentor should stand up and come forward. This is best accomplished by having presenters sit on the opposite side of the room to keep them from bumping into each other as they change positions.

Make sure that all materials are already at the front, so that each presenter does not have to bring their own. You want the audience's attention focused on the person, not on her shuffling of notes, hand-outs, or visual aids. If you are using slides, be sure to insert a blank slide between presenters as a cue.

Keep only one person at the front at a time. Never have two presenters standing at the same time, as this diffuses the audience's attention.

During the question period, have one presenter field the questions and direct them to where the answers are. "That's in Joyce's area. Joyce?" If Joyce answers the question, allow only that one answer.

The key to an effective team presentation is unity. It should flow as smoothly as a presentation by one person. More practice is required up front to effect this unity, but the impact of a team presentation can be very dynamic.

USING VISUAL AIDS SUCCESSFULLY TO ENHANCE YOUR MESSAGE

Hand Outs

Pros. Handouts reinforce your message and leave the audience with something to review.

Cons. If you distribute handouts before or during your presentation, the audience will read them as you talk. A better strategy is to use key points from handouts in your presentation and control what your audience sees. Distribute handouts after your presentation to emphasize key points.

Mechanics. Be sure your complete name, address, and phone number appear on the cover page.

If you have materials — a report, a technical document, etc. — that your audience needs to see before your presentation, send it ahead and use the presentation time to answer questions.

Don't pass around samples unless you have one for everyone. Otherwise you'll lose the attention of audience members as they anticipate receiving the sample, look at the sample, and pass the sample.

Flip Charts

Pros. Flip charts can be very effective because you can write on them as the discussion progresses. They are large enough for up to ten people to see, and they give you a place to draw examples. "A picture is worth a thousand words."

Cons. Flip charts are difficult to carry. It is easier to arrive early and prepare them on site.

Mechanics. For flip charts that build upon one another, tape them to the wall as you go. However, remove the flip chart when you are finished with it to avoid distraction.

Prelined flip-chart paper is easier to write on. Use two colors only. Blue and red are best: blue for the body, red for emphasis (bullets, underlining). Invest in high-quality, broad-tipped felt markers.

In a flip-chart presentation, each page should have a title. For a team presentation, use a standard format and color scheme to achieve unity.

Don't try to squeeze in everything on a page. Keep it simple; by using only key words.

When using a flip chart, plant your feet next to the chart and face the audience, not the chart. Point to it by turning at the waist. Keep eye contact with the audience even while pointing.

The flip chart allows you to reveal only the information you want your audience to see, and it keeps their attention focused on what you are saying.

Overheads (transparencies)	**Pros.** Overheads are a good choice for a audience of twenty or more. They allow you to control what the audience sees and to build a sales case.

Cons. Overheads require special equipment to prepare and project and if framed, may not fit in your briefcase.

Mechanics. The same rules apply to overheads as for all visuals: Don't try to put too much information on one visual; stick to key points: use the two-color scheme for emphasis; and use large letters for maximum visibility.

When pointing to an item on an overhead, point on the projector, not on the screen. Turn off the projector between overheads. This focuses the attention back on you. Overheads that are framed are much easier to handle, and you can make notes right on the frame. |
| **Desktop Easel** | **Pros.** The desktop easel combines the advantages of flip charts and overheads in a small, portable form. It is appropriate with one to five people. Since pages are slid into glassine protectors, it is easy to change their content or order. The prospect sees the front side, and you have a copy on the back side, which faces you. |
| **Slides** | **Pros.** Slides are easy to carry and use, and are relatively low-cost. You can use progressive disclosure with slides; that is, let each slide build upon the one before it.

Cons. To use slides, you must turn off the lights. This may detract from your presentation. Slides require special equipment to prepare and project.

Mechanics. When using slides, stand beside the screen and face the audience. Operate the projector with a remote switch so that you can be in the front of the room. Let the slides support your ideas, and keep talking between slides. |

GUIDELINES FOR USING VISUAL AIDS

1. Never use a visual aid before an audience until you have practiced with it. Be sure your visuals are in the

proper sequence and that you can handle them comfortably. Practice turning the projector on and off.

2. Design the aid to help, not hinder, communication. Each aid should be simple and clear and should demonstrate a single point. Use color for contrast and emphasis. Handle the aid only when making direct reference to it.

3. Don't stand between your audience and the visual aid. Stand to one side, use a pointer, and keep eye contact with the audience.

4. Project your voice. The audience's attention is divided between you and your aid, so you need to speak with more volume than normally required.

5. Keep talking. Use visuals to support what you are saying. Don't interrupt your presentation when changing aids.

WORKSHEET: EFFECTIVE SALES PRESENTATIONS

1. Using the four-point presentation system, decide what you would like to say to your prospects.

Key Idea #1: Benefits

Key Idea #2: The Strengths of Your Bank

Key Idea #3: The Package of Services

Key Idea #4: The Relationship

5 Customer Development

Your prospects don't care how much you know...until they know how much you care.
Gerhard Gschwandtner

"Cross-selling" is the term the banking industry uses to describe the customer development process. If a customer asks for a checking account and you also recommend a savings account, you have cross-sold that savings account. Cross-selling is the activity we use to build customer relationships. Some banks track a cross-sell ratio, which measures how many products you sold compared to how many people you saw.

No matter what you call it or how you measure it, *cross-selling* is just good *selling*. It is a win-win-win situation: The customer wins through the convenience of having all banking accounts in one place and dealing with one banker; the bank wins because it is more profitable to build relationships than to sell accounts, one by one; and *you* win through the satisfaction of knowing that you have helped a customer solve problems and you have supported the strategic objectives of your company.

WHAT CUSTOMERS WANT

Customers have definite ideas about what they want in a bank. They choose a bank based on how well you meet

their expectations. Once you understand their expectations, you are in a position to cross-sell effectively.

Security Customers want to believe that their money is safe. They want to feel confident in their banker. They want their bank to have a stable financial record. It's up to you to establish this picture of security in the customer's mind.

Recognition Customers want you to acknowledge their importance and recognize their value to the bank. They are able to get this recognition from other establishments and expect it from you too. They want to be treated as individuals. You can do this by using their name, remembering small facts about them and their family, and thanking them for their business.

Convenience Your customers are busy, and they want to be able to do their banking in one place, quickly and efficiently. You can make banking convenient for your customers by giving good service, following up thoroughly, and keeping informed about all of your products.

A Competitive Rate Your customers are looking for a good rate. A good rate is determined in relationship to what else is available, the degree of risk involved, and what your competitors are offering. You can *make* a rate competitive by presenting the *value* it represents.

HOT BUTTONS FOR BUSINESSPEOPLE

In addition to the four general interests above, there are particular areas of interest to businesspeople. The more you weave them into your conversation, the more success you will have.

Profit A business can continue only as long as it produces a profit. Virtually every product and service you provide impacts profit. Learn to stress this area when discussing your products. For example:

"Mr. Big, our investment services division can help you not only guard your assets but strengthen your balance sheet, giving you the leverage you'll need to continue your expansion."

"Ms. Big, our account receivables financing will shore up your short-term profits while you lay the groundwork for the summer season."

Production Business owners want their production operations to run smoothly and predictably from day to day. As increasing demands are placed on production, owners look for ways to reduce disruption of the normal routine and increase efficiency. Relate your products to improved production. For example, an equipment loan may produce a dramatic impact on the assembly line by allowing for the purchase of a newer technology.

Growth and Change Business owners want to make sure their operations can handle a growing work load. As technology advances,

they want to keep up with new developments. A line of credit allows them to take advantage of opportunities as they arise.

Cost Control Every business owner wants to keep the lid on costs. Owners look for new and improved methods to monitor, measure, and manage costs. A cash management account allows the customer to invest funds at a high rate until they are needed to meet obligations. A payroll system saves time and money by automating tedious jobs.

Quality of Output Business owners are concerned about the quality of the product or service they provide. They continually seek to develop enhancements that provide greater value for their customers. You can draw a parallel between their concern for quality and the quality you provide as an advisor.

Attracting and Retaining Good Employees Employees are the most significant resource for a business. Owners are interested in developing ways to avoid losing effective employees, especially in locations or job categories with labor shortages. Let them know how direct deposit, IRAs, pension services, and other conveniences can be offered as a benefit to their employees.

Saving Time "Time is money," and the services that save time for that business owner or professional are valuable. Commercial tellers, night deposit, and telephone transfer are just three of the conveniences that are important to businesspeople.

Retirement Security Successful businesspeople want to be assured that all of their hard work will provide a comfortable life after they retire or sell their business. And yet it's easy to get so caught up in today's problems that one forgets to plan ahead. You can provide a valuable service through financial planning aimed at securing their lifestyle. This includes investments, retirement plans, and insurance.

HOT BUTTONS FOR REALTORS

Realtors have specific areas of interest, including:

- Quick turnaround.
- Exclusive listings.
- "No-problem" loans.
- Satisfied customers.
- Increased earnings.
- Flexible programs.
- Good communication with lender.
- Current market information.

Your mortgage options, the personal service you provide, and your efficient processing and servicing of loans all tie in directly to these interests. Talk about the *realtor's* needs and you will be far more successful than if you concentrate on your services alone.

SELLING TO REALTORS

The mortgage lending business has remained a stable source of income for many savings institutions. It has helped them keep their balance sheets strong in a shifting rate environment. Many savings institutions now have an active calling program on realtors. Since a realtor has many options to choose from when advising a home buyer about where to get a mortgage, a banker must make his institution stand out from the crowd.

These four points will help you distinguish your services:

1. **Build a Relationship.** A long-term relationship will be the most profitable for you and your bank. To build one, you must instill *trust,* be seen as *consistent* and *professional,* and provide the best *service* on every deal.

2. **Make It Attractive.** You have to do more than drop off rate sheets. Use these phrases to demonstrate what you can do for the realtor.

   "I understand your needs."
   "We have done this successfully for many years."
   "I can help you be more successful."
   "Let me handle the details."
   "Let me educate your brokers."
   "Let me show you."

Sell your professionalism and competence and the ease of doing business with your bank. Assume success going through the door, and keep going back until you've established a steady stream of business. Remember: They need *you* to help them earn their commission.

3. **Maintain Your Golden Image.** Keep the business you've worked so hard to cultivate by:

   - Doing it right.
   - Doing it on time.
   - Doing it consistently.
   - Keeping informed.
   - Providing all the extras:

     Progress reports.
     Status reports of deals in the works.
     Loan type explanations.
     A checklist of what to expect in processing.
     Updates for agents.
     Broker seminars.

- Showing interest in problems.
- Keeping your backup team primed.
- Being yourself.
- Always following through.

4. **Strive to Do More.** You've got to work *smarter* than the other originators to attract your share of business. Consider these ideas:

- Have you penetrated all the offices in your area?
- Do you know all the brokers?
- Are you available when they need you?
- Have you made a handout for brokers to give clients?
- Will you beat your own best record?

OFFER MORE THAN YOUR COMPETITOR DOES

The originator who only drops off rate sheets and thinks this is a sales call is missing a big opportunity with realtors. There are many more valuable handouts you can use with your clients, including:

1. **Progress Reports.** A progress report lets the realtor know what deals are in progress and the status of each. Produced monthly, it not only keeps him updated but acts as a reminder for all you're doing for him.
2. **Market Update.** Don't underestimate your value as a source of information to the realtor. Prepare quarterly market updates that let him know what's happening in the business and consumer sectors of the local economy.
3. **Outline of Realtor Education.** Demonstrate the value of your new broker seminars by developing a written agenda.
4. **Description of Each Program and Customer Profile.** Provide a short description of each mortgage program and indicate for whom it's intended. This not only helps the buyer but may clear up questions the realtor has.

5. **Handouts for Home Buyers.** As a local institution, you know a lot about your area. Make up a handout for realtors to give their customers that includes things like restaurants, movie theaters, dry cleaners, etc.—anything that makes the move easier for them.

These handouts serve both to educate the realtor and home buyer and to clearly show that you want to provide good service.

Other industry Hot Buttons

- Medical professionals: Collecting receivables.
- Attorneys: Billable versus nonbillable hours.
- Automobile dealers: Inventory turns.

BUILDING CUSTOMER RELATIONSHIPS

Know the Strengths and Services of Your Bank

Before you can successfully communicate your services to a customer, *you* must understand them fully. This means being able to explain your products and services to customers at all levels of sophistication. This gives you credibility.

Knowing the business objectives of your bank is important for you because it helps you know where to invest your time and effort. If you pursue sales that are not consistent with the objectives of your management (this includes making too many goodwill calls), you will probably end up feeling frustrated.

As a professional, you are responsible for understanding the business objectives of your bank so that your sales efforts will be compatible with them.

Know Your Customer's Objectives

Just as understanding your bank's objectives helps you focus your sales strategy, understanding your customer's objectives positions you as a valuable advisor.

Tailor your recommendation to meet your customer's objectives. One way to do this is to use the customer's language in proposals and presentations.

With commercial customers, make a point of keeping updated on their business through regular calling, attendance at business functions, and attention to newspaper articles. Knowing the customer's objectives puts you in the position of being able to satisfy them.

Get to Know the Key People

To build relationships, get to know the key people in your commercial accounts. Many a sale has been lost by not knowing who the right person to talk to was. Don't fall into this trap. Find out who the key people in your potential account are *before* you try to close the sale.

You can find out who these people are in a variety of ways:

- From organization charts.
- In articles in business journals and other periodicals.
- From other bank employees.
- By asking questions.

Asking questions is usually the most effective way of gaining this information. Even if you think you already know whom you need to talk to, it is important to verify that information. People will give you the names you ask for if you have already gained rapport and if your request seems friendly.

At each opportunity try to find out:

- Who actually has the authority to make a decision (decision-maker).
- Who will have the most influence on that decision (key influencer).

The Formal and Informal Organization

There are two organizational forms you should become familiar with. The *formal organization* refers to what is revealed on an organization chart: who reports to whom and what is the management span of control. The *informal organization* refers to the actual alliances and power relationships that exist in the business. Very often the formal organization and the informal organization are quite different; they may even be at odds. Therefore, it takes good observation skills to detect these differences. The more you can learn about the decision-maker, key influencers, the formal organization, and the informal organization, the better position you are in to achieve success with that customer. And of course you can most easily learn these things through frequent calling on your customer.

Learn to Spot Key Events

Part of being attuned to what is going on in your customer's business is learning to recognize key events that may influence your ability to sell new services to that customer.

Examples of key events include: functional reorganizations, promotions, competitive marketing campaigns, budget planning sessions, operating crises, and changes in the company's mission.

Train yourself to look at key events in terms of how they affect your sales strategy. If you have kept an open line of communication with key people in the account, key events provide you with the opportunity to go back to see them, discuss how the event will impact their business, and suggest a product or service that can help. This clearly demonstrates your interest in their business and your professionalism in keeping updated on your customers.

Become a Team Player

Cultivate the image in the customer's mind of your position as a team player: someone working side-by-side with them to help accomplish their goals.

The opposite image is to be characterized as a "pushy salesperson from the bank." Your objective is to make your customer feel that you are genuinely concerned about her needs. Make recommendations, share your views, and use reference selling to build your credibility as an advisor.

Businesspeople are not looking for a bank; banks are a dime a dozen. They are looking for a *banker*. And that banker can be you!

With a commercial customer, it is your responsibility to keep updated on the business so that you will be able to make timely and effective recommendations. The following checklist will help you identify what you need to know about each of your customer accounts. Put a copy of this checklist in each of your customer's files and use it as a guide for collecting information. (See Table 5.1)

TABLE 5.1 Getting to Know a Company

The Business
- ☐ Type of business: wholesale, retail, manufacturer
- ☐ Products they provide
- ☐ Profitability of products
- ☐ Company's target market
- ☐ Company's major competitors
- ☐ Competitive pressures
- ☐ Geographic trading area
- ☐ Key issues in company's industry
- ☐ Effects of changing economy on business
- ☐ Local market conditions and effect on company
- ☐ Length of time in business
- ☐ Size of company: annual sales, net worth, number of employees
- ☐ Complete company name, mailing address, street address, and phone number

TABLE 5.1 continued

- ☐ Type of organization: headquarters, branch office, subsidiary, division
- ☐ Community involvement

The Management

- ☐ Owner and principals
- ☐ Decision-maker (who has the ultimate veto power?)
- ☐ Key influencers (to whom does the decision-maker listen?)
- ☐ Titles and phone numbers of decision-maker and key influencers
- ☐ Decision-maker and key influencers' secretaries' names
- ☐ Chief financial officer
- ☐ Company accountant
- ☐ Company attorney
- ☐ Directors

The Banking Relationship

- ☐ Current relationship with your bank
- ☐ Potential development of the relationship
- ☐ Products and services they use
- ☐ How they use these products and services
- ☐ Bank employees who know decision-maker and key influencer
- ☐ Other similar bank customers (for reference selling)

The Goals

- ☐ Customer's business goals and objectives
- ☐ Constraints affecting business
- ☐ Constraints affecting banking relationships
- ☐ Areas of concern in banking relationships
- ☐ Selection criteria for choosing a bank
- ☐ Time frame for a decision to change a banking relationship
- ☐ Customer's expectations for a banking relationship
- ☐ Customer's expectations of the banker
- ☐ Unusual circumstances in the way they conduct banking business
- ☐ What pleased the decision-maker in past banking relationships
- ☐ What irritates decision-maker in banking relationships
- ☐ What support do they need in financial planning
- ☐ Where are the personal accounts of principals, officers, managers, and employees

WORKSHEET: CUSTOMER DEVELOPMENT

1. Take a moment to reflect on and list your bank's competitive advantages:
   1.   6.
   2.   7.
   3.   8.
   4.   9.
   5.   10.

2. Pick one of your customers and look at the checklist on pages 84 and 85. What facts are you missing? Plan to collect them on your next visit.

3. Review your filing system for prospects and customers. How could you use the checklist to enhance the file?

4. List two of your customers and their hot buttons.

   How could you use this information?

6 Handling Objections

Salesmanship begins when the customer says no!

OBJECTIONS—JUST AN OPPORTUNITY IN DISGUISE

An objection is any fact or feeling—expressed or unexpressed—that a customer has that may cause him not to agree with your recommendation.

Objections may be revealed:

"Your service charge is too high!"
"Your interest rate is too low!"

Objections may be hidden:

("I can't make this decision without jeopardizing my job.")
("I'm uncertain about what to do.")

Objections occur at all stages of the sales cycle. Your customer is telling you that she has a problem with what you are discussing. It is the salesperson's responsibility to resolve the objection before continuing with the discussion.

Rather than something to be dreaded, an objection should be viewed as an opportunity for you to learn more about what your customer wants. An objection tells you exactly what the customer's concerns are so that you will know what areas to focus on. Skill at handling objections comes through practice, but the most important point is to understand the objection before responding.

Try to avoid getting defensive, which will impair your communication ability. Customers have a right to raise objections; it is their way of "checking everything out" so that they will feel secure with their final decision. It is the time during the sales process when you can best demonstrate your problem-solving abilities.

FOUR AREAS FOR OBJECTIONS

Objections always come up around four main points in the sale of any product or service:

1. **Price.** For financial services, this is expressed in terms of rate, fee, or service charge (see Table 6.1).
2. **Performance.** Objections about performance question whether the product or service will actually deliver the advantages promised.
3. **Delivery.** Concerns about delivery refer to the way in which the customer receives the product—for example, whether or not cash transfers are made on the day ordered.
4. **Service.** Service objections refer to such things as whether all checks are returned with statements, loan payments are deducted on the proper day, new check orders arrive in a timely fashion, or mortgage processing is completed in the promised timeframe.

You'll tend to hear the same objections over and over again, so you will want to prepare and think through your responses so you won't get sidetracked.

FOUR-STEP PROCESS FOR HANDLING OBJECTIONS

1. **Pause.** This gives you a chance to collect your thoughts so you won't respond defensively. It will also defuse an emotional situation if the objection was expressed heatedly.

2. **Question.** Verify that you have understood the objection. For example: "Mr. Prospect, are you saying that the fee is higher than the one you're used to or that you don't think it's warranted for this product?"

   It is important that you quickly identify the issue so that you can respond to it. People do not always express things in terms we understand. Therefore, ask a question to verify your understanding of what was said.

3. **Respond.** The response has two parts: an empathy statement that shows that you understand the concern, and an answer to the objection. Your answer may provide information, clear up a misunderstanding, or counteract a negative with benefits.

4. **Verify.** To determine that the objection has been answered to the customer's satisfaction, ask, "Have I put that concern to rest?" You will know if an objection has not been answered when it comes up over and over again or if the call seems to take a "wrong

"ARE YOU SAYING THAT THE SERVICE CHARGE IS HIGHER THAN YOU'RE USED TO, OR THAT YOU DON'T THINK IT'S WARRANTED FOR THE PRODUCT?"

turn." If that happens, go back to the area of concern and re-explain.

Let's see how this process works with a real objection:

Customer: "The interest rate is higher on Hutton's Money Market Account."

Step 1: Pause

Salesperson: "..............."

Step 2: Question

Salesperson: "It that extra ¼ percent important to you?"

Customer: "Well, I like to know all my options."

Salesperson: "There are a lot of products on the market. It can be confusing."

Customer: "You're right. I hear about so many different to invest these days that I'm not really sure what to do."

(You have just learned that the objection is that the customer is confused and looking for reassurance.)

Step 3: Empathy statement

Salesperson: "I can understand your confusion."

Step 3: Respond

Salesperson: "Let me explain our Money Market Account options to you, and then you can decide which is best for you." (Explain options.)

Step 4: Reference-sell to verify: Has objection been answered?

Salesperson: "You know, our accounts are FDIC-insured for up to $100,000, and a lot of our customers enjoy that feeling of security."

Customer: "Well, I like the idea of an insured high-interest account. I'd like to know more about it."

Customer verifies that concern has been put to rest.

Objections can be answered by:

- Explaining something.
- Demonstrating a capability.
- Or referring to how the issue was handled by others.

TABLE 6.1 Beat the Rate Objection with the System Call

Here is a proven successful answer to the rate objection. When a prospect tells you that your rate or fee is too high (or too low) ask the following two questions:

Question 1: "What are you comparing our rate to?"

You may find the prospect is comparing your rate to:

1. A rate that is no longer offered.
2. A rate he saw in a newspaper several weeks ago.
3. A rate a friend may have received for a similar product several weeks before from another bank.
4. A rate he saw or was told about for a different product.
5. A rate he received from your bank a long time ago.

If any of these situations exist, clear up the misunderstanding. If the prospect is indeed comparing apples to apples, you can still beat the rate objection by demonstrating that your rate includes an entire system of services and support that distinguish your product from the competition by asking the following question:

Question 2: "What does their rate include?"

Tell the prospect that your rate includes:

1. Accurate service, correct documents, proper posting.
2. A rate you can count on when we commit to you.
3. Many years of banking and business expertise.
4. Staff professionalism, specialized training, and continuing formal education.
5. The ability and interest in handling all your business.
6. Innovation with new products and new systems to better support your needs.
7. Investment in state-of-the-art technology for better service in the future.
8. Ability to find a solution to fit your needs.
9. A personal commitment to you.
10. A friendly voice on the other end of a problem.

The answer to the rate objection is to show the prospect that you are offering more than just a "stripped-down" product. You offer an entire system of value. You can demonstrate that your product will provide the prospect with the four big benefits: convenience, recognition, security, and a good return on investment. With the System Sell you can show your prospect why your service is the true bargain.

SWITCH-OFF TECHNIQUE

The switch-off technique turns a negative into a positive, and an objection into a buying question.

If you hear:	You might say:
"It costs too much."	"I believe you are really asking how can this be worked into your budget. Is that correct?"
"I want to think about it!"	"I believe you're still wondering why you ought to go ahead today. Is that right?"

REPHRASE TECHNIQUE

When you hear an objection, up to 20 percent of the time it is a smoke screen. This technique allows you to determine if the objective is real or hidden.

If you hear:	You might say:
"I can't afford it."	"Are you saying it's over your budget or you just don't see the value at the current price?"
"It's too risky."	"Do you feel that the risk/reward ratio isn't great enough, or is it that you're not satisfied with the profit potential?"

Sometimes an objection arises from misinformation about your policies. Other times the objection refers to something you cannot change, such as an unfavorable interest rate, which requires an answer from you that clearly shows that the benefits outweigh this negative. Of course you can only *suggest* this—the customer must agree to it (see Table 6.2).

TABLE 6.2 The "Feel-Felt-Found" Technique

The "Feel-Felt-Found" technique is another way to handle an objection. It works like this:

FEEL
"I can understand how you *feel*."

FELT
"Others have *felt* this way."

FOUND
"But they *found* that when they tried us,
our superior service and variety of products worked well for them.
Don't you think you'd feel the same way?"

"I CAN UNDERSTAND HOW YOU **FEEL** OTHERS HAVE **FELT** THIS WAY, BUT THEY **FOUND** THAT WHEN THEY PUT THE PAYROLL SERVICE IN PLACE, THE SAVINGS IN TIME ALONE EASILY JUSTIFIED THE COST."

Sometimes it is difficult to find out what the real objection is. That is why you must continue to test whether the customer is prepared to buy.

DEALING WITH HIDDEN OBJECTIVES

Watch out for these unspoken, but very real, objections:

1. *Fear* of appearing incompetent to handle financial matters.
2. *Concern* that your recommendation is not in the customer's best interest.
3. *Uncertainty* when faced with the wide variety of financial options.
4. *Desire* to control the salesperson.
5. *Resistance* to change.

One clue that you may not have uncovered the real objection is that the expressed objection continues to come up, even though the customer has given you every indication that you answered it successfully. Another clue is that the customer seems to be objecting to *everything* you bring up.

In either of these cases you may not be able to answer the objection directly. If you sense that an issue of personal power is at stake, it is best not to mention it directly—find other ways of satisfying your customer's needs (see Table 6.3).

TABLE 6.3 Guidelines for Dealing Successfully with Objections

---

1. Respect your customer's right to raise objections. Don't show that you are irritated or annoyed by an objection.
2. Never minimize a customer's objection. Although it may seem petty to you, once the objection has been voiced, your customer has a stake in defending it.
3. Don't place the customer on the defensive by challenging the objection. Your role is to understand it and then answer it, calmly and professionally.
4. Don't invite objections with questions like "You don't see any problems with this, do you?" A question like this challenges the customer to come up with a problem to prove that he is following the discussion.

5. Don't persist with verification if it is obvious that the customer is uncomfortable with your questions. Move to another topic, resolving to re-examine the objection later.
6. Never get into an argument with your customer over an objection. In an argument with a customer, even when you "win," you lose.
7. Don't respond to objections with pat answers like "It's bank policy" or "We've always done it that way." Make an attempt to personalize your response.
8. Don't be afraid to tell your customer that you are confused. If you don't understand an objection, you cannot answer it.
9. Don't delay in answering an objection. Your customer will remain fixed on her objection until you answer it.
10. Don't get sidetracked by objections. Once an objection has been answered, move on to the rest of the call.

WORKSHEET: HANDLING OBJECTIONS

List five objections you frequently encounter, and prepare a response for each. Focus on turning a negative into a positive.

1. Objection:

    Response:

2. Objection:

    Response:

3. Objection:

    Response:

4. Objection:

    Response:

5. Objection:

    Response

7 Successful Closing Strategies

> When I feel that what I am selling is really right for someone, that it simply makes sense for this particular customer, I never feel I am imposing. I feel I am doing him a favor.
>
> Mark McCormack, author
> *What They Don't Teach You at Harvard Business School*

Good closes comes from good selling. Closing is just a piece of the process. And your personal style is what makes it work.

The most important part of the sales process is the salesperson. The kind of *salesperson* you are is the kind of *person* you are. You cannot be one kind of person and another kind of salesperson. The prospect must buy *you* before he will buy your ideas and your products. According to the Sales and Marketing Executives Club of New York City, 71 percent of our customers buy from us because they like us, trust us, and respect us.

CLOSING — JUST ONE MORE PIECE OF THE PROCESS

Although closing is the last step in the sales cycle, it is only the beginning of the relationship with your customer. When you have gained his commitment, all the actions you take *then* will influence whether you keep the commitment. A recent study showed that 68 percent of those who have stopped doing business with organizations because of the "lack of concern shown by the employees of the business." That means that closing is the process by which you begin to ensure a long-term relationship.

Everything you have done up to the point of asking for the sale—identifying a prospect, qualifying him, defining his needs, developing his needs to match your products, and proposing a solution—feeds into your close.

You already know how to close if you've ever had a prospect say yes to your suggestion. To help you improve your closing ratio—to get "yes" more easily and more often—you may want to try some of the techniques in this chapter. It takes work to improve your close ratio, but it's worth it. After all, how much commission or career advancement have you experienced from *almost* meeting your sales goals?

FEAR OF CLOSING

One of the biggest problems for salespeople is actually asking for the order. The anxiety associated with asking for customer commitment may prolong the sales process unduly.

Here are several emotions you may feel that prevent you from closing:

- Fear that the prospect will turn you down.
- Uncertainty about whether your product or price is right.
- Uncertainty about how to build agreements throughout the sale or awkwardness in asking for agreement at the end.
- Expecting the prospect to say no.
- Sympathy to the point of becoming negative yourself.

EMPHASIZE QUALITY, VALUE, AND SERVICE

If you have been concerned, professional, empathetic, and convincing, your close will be a logical extension of the sales process and will have a good chance of being successful. When you have been selling throughout your association with the prospect, the close comes as no surprise to either of you—it is your way of letting your prospect in on "the good stuff" as soon as possible.

Closing is an *educational* process through which you raise the value of the product in the prospect's mind. Until the value is equal to or greater than the price/rate/fee in the prospect's mind, no sale will be made.

The purpose of the close is to help the prospect forget price/rate/fee and remember *quality, value,* and *service*.

LAYING THE GROUNDWORK FOR THE CLOSE

You can lay the groundwork for a successful close by seeking out what your prospect needs and wants. People only buy what they need and want. And we all know that money can be found for those things we truly want. Your job is to find out what that prospect wants and help him get it.

By asking open questions, observing the prospect's behavior, and using your knowledge of other customers as a guide, you can provide a truly customized solution for each prospect. And once you've done that, the close only requires the prospect's approval to get started.

Think of yourself as a problem solver. Dispensing information is not selling. Selling requires persuasion. You can't necessarily close just because you have good product knowledge.

GOING AFTER TOP PEOPLE WITH CONFIDENCE AND A POSITIVE ATTITUDE

If you feel comfortable dealing with a first-line supervisor but get cold feet if you have to talk to a vice president, consider this: that vice president may just be wondering why you never come to see *her*!

Your fear is probably based on assumptions like "She doesn't have time," "She wouldn't be interested," or "She'll just refer me down the line." The fact may be that she would be flattered to be singled out by your attention.

If you truly believe in your company and its products and you are convinced of the advantages your products will give her business, then you have an obligation to keep the top people in the account informed. This does not mean that you deal in details with the executive management team. What it does mean, however, is that you let them know that you are interested in their business problems and that you are proposing solutions for them.

This communication may take the form of an initial introduction call, at which you explain your bank's services and discuss other businesses you've worked with. It may include periodic visits to inform top management of new services. It may be a phone call every now and then to find out if she has any questions or if she is satisfied with your service.

However you manage to keep the executive management team of the account informed, it should be done with the complete confidence that it is an integral part of the customer development process.

THE BUY SIGNAL: VERBAL AND NONVERBAL

Many salespeople ask, "When is the right time to close?" The answer is simple: when you get a buy signal. A buy signal is any indication from the prospect that he desires your product or service.

Verbal buy signals are expressed by the prospect directly:

"How much money will I save?"
"Can I get the approval by Monday?"
"How soon can we get started?"
"Will you be here to help us with the new product?"
"Let's go in together to see Mr. Big."
"I want to do business with you."

Buy signals may be nonverbal, requiring close attention to discern:

- An eager look.
- Leaning forward.
- Rapid nodding.
- A broad smile.
- The end of a line of questioning.
- A move by the prospect to collect all the papers you have been going over.
- A friendly glance toward the decision-maker by his key advisors.

Buy signals are opportunities to close. Listen carefully for them with your prospects.

THE TRIAL CLOSE

The secret to having a high close ratio is trying to close early and often. A trial close allows you to try to gain the prospect's commitment at any point during the sales call. Trial closes help you find the areas of agreement and narrow down the areas that require additional persuasion on your part. Here is an example of a trial close:

Prospect: "Can I get customized checks?"
Salesperson: "If I can have them for you by next Friday, would you open the account today?"

Notice the strategy of "If I can..., would you...?" Depending on the prospect's answer, the salesperson knows exactly where he must go next in the sales call.

Trial closes help you keep focused on your objective—to sell—and help the prospect reach a satisfying decision early.

CLOSING STRATEGIES THAT GET RESULTS

You can sell more by asking than by telling. Good closes put the ball in the prospect's lap by asking a question and forcing a decision.

Following are seven closes that can help you persuade more people to take action in their own best interest. They work, but only if you use them!

Alternative Close
The Alternative Close lets your prospect choose between something and something else ("Would you like this one or that one?"), rather than between something and nothing ("Would you like to go with this product?").

The Alternative Close assumes the prospect will say yes to the main idea and focuses instead on a "detail" of the sale.

"Would deposits every month or twice a month work best for you?"
"Would you like to invest 100 percent or 75 percent in the five-year CD?"
"Will you be assigning check-signing privileges to Jane and Jim or just to Jane?"
"Would a line of $15,000 or $20,000 make more sense to you at this point?"

Three-Question Close
The Three-Question Close is very effective in many situations. It basically works like this:

1. "Can you see how this would save you money (time)?"
2. "Are you interested in saving money (time)?"
3. "If you were ever going to start saving money (time), when do you think would be the best time to start?"

By getting the prospect to agree that he sees *and* wants the benefit, you help him decide that *now* is the time to get started. And by asking the questions, you are allowing the prospect to make the decision himself.

Affordable Close

The Affordable Close is a way for you to help your prospect make a decision in her best interest when she is hesitant due to price/rate/fee.

Break the investment (never the cost) into smaller parts so your prospect can afford it. Make it easy for her to buy.

> "For $50 a week you can build that savings you'll need if you get started now. Most of us don't have the luxury of a substantial nest egg to begin with, but we can build one painlessly with a planned savings strategy."

Another variation of this close works when you are trying to persuade the prospect to invest more than she had intended, such as buying a house in a higher price range or investing in an instrument that requires a certain minimum amount.

Focus your persuasion only on the additional cost: the amount over and above the original amount she had intended to invest. Consider the original investment as sold, and work on the incremental investment.

> "If you look at this investment over a thirty-year period, it only represents an additional $2,000 per year. And even if your salary stays the same—and of course it won't—that only means an extra $167 per month, or $5.57 a day. And wouldn't you agree that the satisfaction and happiness you'll get from your home is well worth the additional $5 a day?"

Assumptive Close

In using the Assumptive Close, the salesperson assumes the prospect will buy and sets up a picture of the satisfaction he will have as the owner of the product.

"Once you have the cash management system installed, you will be free to work on other projects."

The image the businessperson gets is one of himself as less hassled and able to do more interesting work.

"The growth you'll experience with this building expansion loan is right on target for your business plan, isn't it?"

The image the businessowner gets is more success for his business. Tie this close into his objectives.

The Ben Franklin Close

Ben Franklin once said:

"When confronted with two courses of action I jot down on a piece of paper all the arguments in favor of each one—then on the opposite side I write the arguments against each one. Then by weighing the arguments pro and con and canceling them out, one against the other, I take the course indicated by what remains."

The Ben Franklin Close is a "plus-and-minus" list of product features and benefits you create with the customer.

The most effective use of this technique is to create the list visually, on a flip chart or a notepad. Divide a piece of paper vertically in half and label the left-hand column "minus" (-) and the right-hand column "plus" (+). (People tend to remember things on the right-hand side of a page much more often than on the left.)

Next, list the positive points (benefits) on the right as you say them aloud. Use the word "agree."

"Mr. Dentist, we've agreed that you'll earn an additional $200 per month by investing in our Super Account. The growth of your savings and the ease of the automatic

cash transfers provide you with a profitable cash management system. Our hotline lets you change the procedure at any time. You've agreed that this system will give you more time to devote to your practice, giving you the opportunity to achieve your business objectives."

Next, list the negative points on the left-hand side as you say them aloud.

"Mr. Dentist, it's true that you'll be paying ¼ percent higher interest. The monthly fee for maintenance represents an additional charge to you."

The resulting charge looks like this:

−	+
¼ percent interest Monthly fee	$200/month earnings Growth Ease of transfers Hotline Opportunity Business growth No more worry!

SUCCESSFUL CLOSING STRATEGIES

Now, point to the chart and say, "Wouldn't you agree that the advantages to you of opening a Super Account far outweigh these points?" Of course, make sure you have more entries under "+" than under "–"!

This technique can be quite useful in helping the hesitant prospect come to a decision. Seeing it in black and white can be very reassuring.

A more aggressive use of this method is to fill out the plus side and hand the prospect your pen and ask him to fill out the minus side. Sometimes this is enough to help him see that his objections are minimal compared to the advantages. It will also help you to quickly determine if this prospect is indeed worth following through with.

The "If I could, would you?" Close

This close can quickly qualify a prospect as a buyer or a "tire-kicker." It is especially useful with the prospect who asks a lot of questions about details.

It works like this:

> Prospect: "Can I use the loan privilege right away?"
> Salesperson: "If I could get the loan approved for you today, would you open the account?"

By the process of elimination, you can test each of the prospect's concerns in this way. You will know that you have found his hot button when he answers yes to your questions.

It can also be used in this way:

Prospect: "Your rate is higher than the Z Bank."
Salesperson: "If our rates were the same, whom would you choose?"
Prospect: "You."
Salesperson: "Then aren't you saying that you recognize that our products are superior? Don't sell yourself short by focusing only on rate."

This close is the most direct way to determine the prospect's buying criteria.

Agreement Close

By gaining the prospect's agreement throughout the sales process, the salesperson sets the climate for the Agreement Close.

The Agreement Close is a selective recitation by you of the agreements you and the prospect have reached together during the sales cycle. It helps the prospect focus on the decision at hand by positively reinforcing his inclinations toward your product.

The Agreement Close is engineered from the beginning by summarizing frequently with the prospect about the points he's agreed to. Then the close becomes just an extension of previous agreements. The salesperson might say:

"We've *agreed*, Mr. Customer, that overall you'll be earning a greater return on your money and that our Super Account meets your working capital requirements. You've also *suggested* that the location of our branch office is much more convenient for you. And you've *agreed* that our response to your request for recommendations in your cash flow planning helped you tremendously last month. I'd like to begin with you today as your personal banker. Wouldn't you *agree* that it's time to open the account?"

The Agreement Close is a very powerful technique for urging the prospect toward an early commitment. The salesperson sets up an autosuggestion condition of mental yes's that is hard for the prospect to resist.

One-Problem Close

The One-Problem Close is appropriate with the prospect who has responded to previous trial closes with: "I want to think it over." This phrase, although discouraging to some, is actually a golden opportunity for you to find out exactly what you have to do to sell the prospect.

The technique is to narrow the prospect down to the major obstacle. It works like this:

Prospect: "I need to think it over."
Salesperson: "I can understand how you feel. Many of our customers felt the same way at this point. I'm sure you still have questions you'd like answered before making a decision, don't you?"
Prospect: "Well, yes, I do."
Salesperson: "Let's make a list of some of them." (List the points of concern as the prospect expresses them.) "Which of these is actually keeping you from going ahead?"

Next, handle this objection and close. This helps the prospect clarify his thoughts about the product.

IF AT FIRST YOU DON'T SUCCEED...

The average sale is made on the fifth try, so if you're only asking once or twice, you're missing out on success that could be yours.

Many prospects do not know what they want because they do not know what is available. So if you cannot fit the bill exactly, do not assume that they are so adamant they would not even consider anything else. Use your imagination to help the prospect get what he or she wants.

People change, situations change, needs arise—you just never know unless you stay in touch. Don't lose a

TABLE 7.1 Closes to Avoid

1. "Can you think of any reason not to go with our service?"
   (Watch out! You've just challenged him, and he'll probably respond with a reason.)
2. "It's obvious everyone else is going with this new type of account. Don't you think it's about time you did?"
   (Translation: "Mr. Customer, your judgment has been poor in the past, but I'm giving you the opportunity to wise up.")
3. "It's the end of the year, and I could really use the commission. Won't you help me out?"
   (If you are that desperate, have enough pride not to let the customer know it! It is not his responsibility to keep you employed!)
4. "There is no risk in this situation for you. Nothing could possibly go wrong. You have my guarantee that you will never have a moment of dissatisfaction."
   (Do you really want to live up to that statement? Avoid the oversell!)
5. "You know, Joe, if you make improvements to the business by signing up for this loan, you're sure to get a promotion."
   (How do you know? This is overstepping your bounds.)

sale because you didn't persist. If you want the business, you have to go after it—as many times as it takes to be successful.

In most cases you cannot significantly change the rate or the fee, but you can dramatically change the *value*. You can educate the customer to the value he or she will receive by providing additional information. That's why you never want to tell it all up front. Save a piece of information about value in case you need it to try to close again or to reinforce the sale after the close. By giving additional information, you are building a relationship based on trust and good communication.

Sometimes, no matter what you do, the prospect will not commit. You often get a feeling that there is more going on than meets the eye in these situations. The best strategy I know when this happens is to look your prospect in the eye and ask, "What do I have to do to get your business?"

The beauty of this technique is that you always find out, even if the answer is "Nothing." Look for ways to use this question early in a sales call. It can save you a tremendous amount of time in a competitive situation.

HOW TO RESTRATEGIZE WHEN YOUR CLOSE FAILS

Trial closes are called "trial" because they are meant to test the waters. When they "fail," this just means that the prospect is not yet ready to commit.

So what do you do? Help him get ready! Use the prospect's response to your trial close to continue qualifying and urging him toward a buying decision.

Successful salespeople restrategize using this new information. It usually takes five tries to close a sale, so if you can get it on the second or third try, you are well ahead of the game. It works like this:

Salesperson:	(Agreement Close.) "You've agreed that the Super Account will make your cash management a lot simpler. The automatic transfers will give you the cash flow you need for placing your orders. If you'll approve this agreement, we can begin working with you immediately."
Prospect:	(Hesitation.) "Well, I don't know. The National Bank has an account that seems similar, and they give free checking."
Salesperson:	(Verify validity of objection.) "Are you saying that free checking is important to you?"
Prospect:	"I think it is a good deal, especially considering the amount of money we would be depositing."

Salesperson: (Minimize objection by stressing relevant benefits.) "Let's look at the entire picture for a moment, Mr. Customer. Our Super Account satisfies your need to have access to your funds at all times. You've agreed that is a very important consideration in your business. Our expert financial counseling could help you plan for your slow seasons while taking advantage of the excess cash to rebuild your inventory for summer. And you mentioned that our branch office was very convenient for your bookkeeper.

"Mr. Customer, wouldn't you agree that the savings, security, credit and opportunity we can give your business far outweigh the free checking?"

Prospect: "You really do offer exactly what I need. And I'm impressed with your knowledge of my business.

"Let's get started. I want to plan for my materials purchases while I'm here today."

Salesperson: "Great! I have everything ready for you."

Restrategizing when your close fails is a matter of listening closely to what your prospect says and formulating a reply that alleviates his concerns.

WORDS THAT SELL

According to several sources, there are certain words that encourage people to do business with you by creating a positive environment. Get out your dictionary and read about all the powerful meanings behind these words, and then start using them in your conversations with customers:

Prospect's name	Proven	Health
Easy	Understand	Money
Safety	Save	New
Discovery	Right	Results
Truth	Profit	Deserve
Happy	Trust	Value
Security	Vital	Advantage
Benefits	Positive	Guarantee
Proud	You	Success
Fun	Love	Comfort

Keep in mind that it's easier to make a *deposit* each month than it is to make a payment; and everyone wants to *invest* money, rather than spend it.

Use these words to create a picture in the prospect's mind of how successful she will be with your product. People don't buy products; they buy how they imagine using them will make them feel.

WORDS THAT ALIENATE

Just as there are words that excite your prospect, there are words that will turn your prospect off. These are words that we have learned to associate with negative implications.

Deal	Cost	I
Pay	Contract	Worry
Try	Mine	Sign
Lose	Hurt	Loss
Death	Bad	Buy
Sold	Price	Sell
Hard	Difficult	Decision
Obligation	Liable	Fail
Failure	Me, My	Liability

Why work against yourself? Avoid the use of these words and insert, instead, more positive words.

TABLE 7.2 Handling Rejection

1. Face it.
Acknowledge the feelings with that rejection: frustration, irritation, anger. Don't try to pretend they don't exist. Of course they exist—that's the mark of a good salesperson. You've put enough of yourself into a sale that you care when things don't work out.

2. Trace it.
Analyze what went wrong. Go back through the sales cycle and determine what you would do differently the next time.

3. Erase it.
Whether failure to make the sale was a result of something you did or did not do, or was the result of some uncontrollable situation, move on to the next prospect. Dwelling on failure increases your chance of failing again. Forget about it! Move on to the next challenge. *Activity overcomes depression.*

SELLING TO DIFFICULT PROSPECTS

Indecisive The indecisive buyer is unsure and afraid to make a mistake. He doesn't like to take a risk, which includes doing *anything* new. This uncertainty causes him to lose out on the benefits of the product.

Your strategy: Win his confidence by showing empathy and reassuring him that he is making the right decision. Your own conviction and belief in your product will be the determining factors. He needs a push — so push him, firmly and with conviction.

Skeptical

The skeptical buyer is always looking at that one little point and wondering if it is truly so. She prides herself on having enough information "not to get taken."

It's best to let this prospect vent her feelings and not argue or contradict her, which would only encourage more skepticism. She wants to be right, and she wants to be understood.

Your strategy: "I'm glad you raised that question, and I want to make sure I understand you clearly. Would you mind repeating it?"

This shows your honest effort to be fair and that you place importance on her words. It also gives the prospect a chance to get out her negative feelings.

After she has expressed her area of doubt, try: "Your question shows me what a quick grasp of the subject you have. It really gets to the heart of the matter, and that's where I'm thinking. We're on the same plane." Then go on to explain.

Hostile

It's important to recognize that people are hostile for a reason, whether or not it has anything to do with you. They are responding to *something*. Just let them talk and vent their hostility. If you allow yourself to get defensive, too, nothing will be accomplished.

Your strategy: "I know exactly how you feel. Others in the past have felt the same way. They found that when they had all the facts, this was the right way for them. I'm pleased you bring your concerns forward in such an open manner, so that I can answer *your* questions too."

This kind of positive statement of their behavior allows your prospect to keep his self-respect and to see himself as reasonable. (No one wants another person to help him see himself as unreasonable!)

In a Hurry This prospect never has the time to hear all the details. She just wants the facts. She is often more interested in saving the time than in saving money.

Your strategy: Be brief, businesslike, and to the point. Handle the sale quickly and save the paperwork for later. Persuade her with bottomline benefits: "Over two years, you will have saved $10,000 with this plan." Leave out the details that can be covered in a follow-up letter.

THE SECRETS OF CLOSING

Conviction: Believe in your bank and its products.

Look for opportunities: Become aware of the customer's needs.

Open the door: Get your prospect talking with open questions.

Success: Expect to win every time.

Education: Learn everything you can about selling and use it.

WORKSHEET: SUCCESSFUL CLOSING STRATEGIES

1. Think back to a sales situation you've been in where the prospect decided *not* to go with your bank. Write that customer's name here:_____
Did you *ask* for the business, or did you present the products and just wait? Often, if we don't ask, they don't volunteer.

2. Which of the closing strategies could you use to be more successful? Resolve to try them in your next few calls.

3. What closing strategies have you heard that you want to avoid using?

8 Successful Communication Skills

Nobody ever listened himself out of a sale.

Opportunity is often missed because we are broadcasting when we should be tuning in.

POOR LISTENING CAN PREVENT SUCCESS

Poor listening can prevent your success in many ways. For example:

1. It can cause you to get the facts wrong.
2. It can render your sales plan useless by causing you to develop it around incorrect information.
3. It can ruin your credibility by causing you to forget important facts.
4. It can cause you to violate protocol because you did not pick up on the politics in the customer account.

Poor listening will negate every positive action you take if it continues long enough.

Effective listening is a key skill for success in selling. If you can learn to listen to what your customers are saying, you will gain a wealth of information that will help you achieve success (see Table 8.1).

TABLE 8.1 Guidelines for Effective Listening

1. Stop talking: You cannot listen if you are talking.
2. Put the speaker at ease: Establish an agreeable atmosphere.
3. Show the speaker that you want to listen: Look and act interested; listen to understand, not to oppose.
4. Remove distractions: Don't doodle, tap, take phone calls, or shuffle paper.
5. Empathize with the speaker: Try to see his/her point of view by putting yourself in the speaker's place.
6. Be patient: Don't interrupt or finish the speaker's sentence.
7. Hold your temper: Emotions result in getting the wrong meanings from words.
8. Ask questions: This shows that you are listening and increases your comprehension.
9. Avoid getting mentally sidetracked: Try to focus on the essence of the topic.
10. Paraphrase what you have heard: This determines if what you understood is actually what the speaker meant.

ACTIVE LISTENING

Active listening refers to the process in which you as the listener not only hear what is being said, but "hear" the *unsaid* message as well. This "listening" occurs through your observation of the speaker's body language, tone of voice, expression, and any other nonverbal cues she gives.

Active listening is a two-way communication. The four characteristics of an active listener are:

1. **Eye Contact.** Give visual feedback to your customer. This does not mean staring—which can be uncomfortable—but visual attentiveness. When, as speakers, we don't get eye contact, we wonder if the other person is listening. Eye contact creates a bond and shows you are interested.

2. **Attentive Behavior.** Lean toward the customer and nod occasionally to show attentiveness. But do not

violate the eighteen-inch personal zone most people like to maintain around themselves. If you lean in too far, you may see a change in your customer's behavior. Leaning forward, nodding, and saying "Uh-huh" show that you care.

3. "You" Questions. Probe with questions that are focused on the listener:

- "*You* did?"
- "What did *you* do next?"
- "How did *you* feel then?"

4. Acceptance. Show that you accept the speaker with a smile and a friendly face. That way, she will feel free to open up to you.

Active listening doesn't imply that you agree with the customer, only that you are listening. Certain vocal expressions, such as "Uh-huh," "I see," and "I understand," also let her know that you are listening. Other indications of your attentiveness are patience and an acceptance of pauses.

Arguing has the opposite effect of listening. It blocks the expression of feelings. If the customer's every point is challenged, she will retreat into a defensive posture. On the other hand, if you demonstrate a desire to understand, the customer will be more inclined to express her feelings.

Any indication of doubt, surprise, disagreement, or criticism will be perceived by your customer as judgment. Judging stimulates defensive behavior. The active listener does not judge. She merely listens.

Indications of agreement and sympathy are usually perceived as support for the customer's point. As a salesperson, you must be careful not to show support for the customer when she suggests reasons not to sign up for a new high-yield account: "The interest rate is not guaranteed" or "I'm not sure this is the best possible alternative." (If you agree with the customer's points, then what are you doing there?)

WHAT MOTIVATES YOUR CUSTOMERS?

People can be categorized as being primarily motivated in one of three ways. As you review these, consider your own motivations and those of your major customers.

Affiliator: "People Who Need People"

Needs to be liked
Warm and friendly
Wants everyone to be able to express their opinions
Wants to be part of the group
Gets confirmation for own beliefs from others
Prefers conciliation; dislikes conflict

Achiever: "Climb Every Mountain"

Concerned with excellence
Gives complete involvement
Expects complete involvement
Looks for unique contributions from others

Competitive
Restless
Innovative
Wants to outdo others
Seeks perfection in tasks
Takes calculated risks
Wants concrete feedback
Goal-oriented
Likes to take personal responsibility

Influencer: "They Did It My Way"

Obtains and exercises power and authority
Verbally fluent
Pushes for acceptance of his ideas
Not content unless everyone agrees
Hard to keep quiet in a meeting
Self-confident
Wants to have an impact on others

How can you use this information with *your* prospects and customers?

BARRIERS TO SUCCESSFUL COMMUNICATIONS

Successful communication occurs when a message is sent and the receiver hears it and understands it. However, many things can prevent successful communication. These barriers include:

1. **Not Listening.** Hearing what someone says is not the same as listening. Many times, when someone else is speaking, we are just waiting to speak, rather than listening.

2. **Assumptions.** When we assume something, our mind is already made up. This influences our ability to effectively understand what the other person is trying to get across.

3. **Details.** Too many details detract from the main message. As a speaker, try to stick to key points and keep details to a minimum. As a listener, try to pick out the key words and take notes to enhance your understanding.

4. **Programming.** In addition to what we hear, we bring in what we already know. This is called programming. It can distort the intended message by giving it a different meaning.

5. **Value Judgments.** Value judgments classify ideas into already-known categories, before the speaker finishes. Expressed value judgments cause the speaker to become defensive and to withhold information.

6. **Environmental Distractions.** Environmental distractions include noise, bright lights, dim lights, uncomfortable seating or temperature, too many or cluttered visual aids, fidgeting audience members, and anything else in the surroundings that makes it difficult to concentrate on the message.

7. **Physical Distractions.** Physical distractions can inhibit communication by focusing attention on something other than the message. These distractions include hunger, poor eyesight, impaired hearing, illness, and anxiety.

8. **Jargon.** Language itself can be a barrier to successful communication if it is used in such a way as to detract from the message. Language barriers include the use of jargon, complex sentence structures, technical terms, acronyms, and grammatical errors. In effective communication, language—your choice of words and sentence structure—is supposed to enhance the listener's understanding of the message, not prove mental superiority.

As the salesperson, it is your job to remove these barriers so that you can concentrate your energies fully on building a relationship with your customer.

BUILDING A POSITIVE COMMUNICATION STYLE

Achieving a positive communication style is the result of self-analysis and practice. Very few of us can do it naturally in all situations.

Take a good, hard look at yourself. What does your appearance say about you? Does your clothing project the image you desire? Are *you* someone you would like to meet?

When a potential customer sees you for the first time, he or she is evaluating *you* as much as your products. This evaluation of you sets the tone for the relationship that follows.

A positive communication style comes from using these key points to give the following messages:

Key Points	*Message Conveyed*
1. Appropriate appearance.	"I am worth your time." "I am a professional."
2. Friendly demeanor.	"I am pleasant to work with." "I can get along with your people."

3. Self-confidence. "I know I can do the job."

4. Active listening. "I think what you are saying is important."
"I will pay attention to your needs."

5. Clear verbal expression. "I am competent."

6. Clear written communication. "I am organized."
"I pay attention to detail."

7. Sensitivity. "I understand your problems and frustrations."
"I share your excitement."
"I won't push you harder than you can take."

KEY IDEAS

WORKSHEET: SUCCESSFUL COMMUNICATION SKILLS

1. How do you feel when someone really listens to you? How can you use the information on active listening to help you in your selling efforts?

2. Prospects/customers I'm currently working with:
   Affiliators
   1.
   2.
   3.
   Achievers
   1.
   2.
   3.
   Influencers
   1.
   2.
   3.

3. Think back to a customer situation you've been involved in during the past month where there was a barrier to communication. What was the barrier? How did it prevent complete understanding?
   What did you do?

9 Telephone Selling

> You can make more friends in two months by becoming really interested in other people than you can in two years by trying to get other people interested in you.
>
> *Dale Carnegie*

The telephone is a magical device. For just a few cents, you can project an image of yourself and your firm to anyone, anywhere in the world. More and more businesses are turning to telephone selling as an alternative to high cost of face-to-face selling. Your first "visit" to a customer may be via the telephone. This first call is the most important one you can make because it establishes the customer's first impression of you. Preparation for this type of sales contact is just as important as the preparation you would put into an on-site sales call. To be successful in telephone selling, you need a system, a structure, and a basic script.

OPPORTUNITIES FOR TELEPHONE SELLING

Telephone selling is a cost-effective strategy for increasing your sales. You can use it in any of the stages of selling to save time and money.

Telephone selling allows you to:

- Increase selling time without additional travel or hours.

"By making some calls before I leave the office, I can save myself a lot of time."

- Improve on-site calls through pre-call qualification.
- Close without having to make an on-site call.
- Reserve on-site calls for high-profit sales.

Telephone selling can be used throughout the sales cycle to:

- Close the sale.
- Secure a potential account.
- Bring you to their attention.
- Identify quality business.
- Determine a prospect's needs.
- Gain information
- Identify the decision-maker.
- Whet their appetite.
- Get a referral.
- Establish an area of mutual interest.
- Qualify a sales lead.

It can also help you with account maintenance:

- Renewals.
- Customer problem resolution.
- Marginal account management.
- Cross-selling.

Telephone selling is a part of a well-integrated sales strategy. Whether you use the phone as a primary sales tool or to supplement your on-site calls, it is a valuable part of your plan for success (see Table 9.1).

TELEPHONE SELLING AS A PRIMARY SALES STRATEGY

If you sell 100 percent of the time over the phone, there are many benefits:

1. **Speed.** In the time it takes you to make a phone call, you have the information you need.
2. **Assurance of Contact.** You can be assured that you will reach someone at the business or home you are

TABLE 9.1 The Telephone in the Sales Cycle

Sales Cycle Stage	Use of the Telephone
Identify	To get a name.

"We offer investment services for companies like yours. With whom should I be talking?"

Qualify	To determine if a sales call is appropriate.
	To determine who the decision-maker is.

"Have you taken advantage of the savings our Cash Management Account offers to businesses like yours?"

"Would you be the person involved in the annual review of your bank relationships?"

Define Needs	To understand their concerns, challenges, and special interests.

"Tell me what you look for in a bank."

Develop Needs	To clarify their needs so you can refine your recommendations.

"June, I'll be sending you the Action Plan for the payroll system, and I just want to verify the number of employees."

"Will Mrs. Smith be named as beneficiary on this account?"

Propose	To gain agreement and get a commitment.

"John, wouldn't you agree that this way of handling your investments makes a lot of sense?"

Close	To follow up and make sure your customer is satisfied.

"I just wanted to check in with you and see how your payroll system is working out."

calling, unlike the mail, where you never know if it arrived or was looked at.

3. **Interaction with Your Prospect or Customer.** This gives you the opportunity to learn new information, answer questions, and handle objections.

4. **Flexibility.** You can quickly react to what your prospect is saying. There is no time delay. When you learn new information, you can "change course."

TELEPHONE SELLING AS A SUPPLEMENTAL SALES STRATEGY

If your primary sales responsibility is face-to-face, you can use telephone selling as a supplemental strategy to:

1. **Convert a Lead into a Sale.** You wouldn't want to spend the time making an on-site call on everyone who only requests information.

2. **Follow Up with Someone Who did not Respond to a Direct-Mail Campaign.** "Hello, this is Jane Jones calling from First National. We have an opportunity for an investment that is yielding 10 percent and we mailed some information to you. I was wondering if you received it and if you would like to take advantage of this opportunity?" This simple approach will

give you the opportunity to create interest where there was none previously.

3. **Manage Your Accounts.** Once a customer has been established, many of the "routine" items can be taken care of by phone. The customer will appreciate your thoroughness and your not being on the scene too often. There is a happy medium between being unresponsive and being overly attentive.

WHEN TO ORGANIZE A TELEPHONE SELLING CAMPAIGN

A telephone selling campaign can be an effective sales strategy anytime. It can help you avoid a sales slump, help you better prepare for an on-site sales presentation, and help you develop more confidence in your selling skills. It also keeps you fresh, as you stay in contact with prospects and customers and learn what is going on in their businesses.

Here are ten reasons to conduct a telephone selling campaign:

1. **Leads Supplied to You.** You have been given several sales leads. You have no idea which are hot and which are not. The simplest and fastest way to determine this is to pick up the phone.

2. **Industry focus.** This is when you organize your telephone selling campaign by industry, calling all the computer firms or all the lawyers in your city. This allows you to profit from your knowledge of a specific group's needs and interests and to use reference selling.

3. **Geographic focus.** You may choose to call all the people in a particular area as a way of segmenting your prospect base and planning your travel.

4. **Position Focus.** A telephone selling campaign can be directed at a certain individual and his interests, such as Treasurer, Pension Plan Manager, or Office Manager.

5. **New-Product Announcement.** A new product is always a good reason to get back in touch with your customers or to contact prospects. If you have done your homework ahead of time and know how that product fits into their business, you can function as an advisor.
6. **New Territory.** A new sales territory is an opportunity to contact customers and prospects to introduce yourself.
7. **Revitalize Sales Performance.** It's easy to get absorbed in "after-sale" activities. You may find yourself at times spending most of your day servicing current accounts. A telephone selling campaign can revitalize your sales performance by adding new prospects to your active list. The more people you contact, the more people you will sell.
8. **Begin a New Week, New Month, New Year.** The start of a new sales period provides an opportunity to start fresh in contacting prospects. Since telephone selling should be a part of any well-integrated sales job, you may want to set aside a specific time each week or each month strictly for telephone selling.
9. **New Job.** When you have a new position in your organization, it's a good time to reconnect with your current customers and new prospects.
10. **Add-On Products.** Products like insurance, credit cards, travelers checks, and CD renewals lend themselves to telephone sales.

INSURING A POSITIVE RESPONSE

How people respond to us on the telephone is affected by many things. To "cause" a positive response, you may want to consider these facts:

1. **People are Primarily Interested in Themselves.** They will respond more favorably to you if you talk in terms of *their* needs and problems.

2. **Everyone Wants to Feel Right and Understood.** If your prospect objects, help him feel understood and right while still correcting his misperception.
3. **We All Respond to the Appeal of Curiosity.** Each of us has a desire to learn. By making statements of benefit to the customer, you appeal to her sense of curiosity.
4. **People Respond to the Pygmalion Effect.** What you expect your prospects to be, they are more likely to be. You should be expecting them to say yes, or else why bother to call? We all respond to the self-fulfilling prophecy. Let them know you want to do more business with them.
5. **People are Goal-Oriented.** All human beings think in terms of goals, things they want to achieve for themselves. If we talk to prospects in terms of *their* goals, it's easy to get their interest.
6. **People Like Pictures.** People think in terms of pictures, not words. Studies have shown that the average child under the age of eleven has an attention span of up to six seconds. They listen and move on—listen and move on.

When adults were tested, do you know what their attention span was? Zero to eight seconds! We would expect that an adult's attention span would be much longer than that of children, but it just isn't so. Our prospects will hear what we have to say and then move on—unless something is done to stimulate their continued interest. Painting pictures and mental images of success with your words will capture your prospect's attention (see Table 9.2).

GETTING THROUGH TO THE DECISION MAKER

Unless you are talking to the right person, you may be wasting your time. The right person is the one who can make the decision. There is always one final decision-maker, even though many others may influence the decision. When in doubt, always start with the president of the company and let him or her refer you down to the

TABLE 9.2 Five Success Tips for Telephone Selling

1. **Identify yourself.**
   Let the caller know right away who you are and where you're from.

2. **Get to the point quickly.**
   Let the caller know why you are calling. What's in it for him?

3. **Show that you are listening.**
   Paraphrase (the verbal equivalent of a nod) to show that you are paying attention.

4. **Create an image of success for the prospect.**
   Paint a picture in his mind with your words. (Refer back to "Words That Sell" in Chapter 7.)

5. **Use the prospect's name.**
   This is a subtle form of recognition that makes the prospect feel important.

---

appropriate person. It is always easier to descend the corporate ladder in selling than to ascend it!

You may encounter the following barriers in getting through to the decision-maker:

1. **Wrong Time of Day—Decision-Maker Not Available.** Ask the receptionist, "What's a good time to catch her?" You may find that 8:00 A.M. or 6:00 P.M. is an ideal time. Try to create a "sales call" by saying, "Please let Mrs. Jones know that I will be calling her tomorrow at 8.00."

2. **Secretary Screening the Call.** Realize that he is doing his job and politely try, "I appreciate your interest, Mr. Smith. I am calling to tell Ms. Jones about the cash management services we offer that are saving thousands of dollars each year for other companies in the area. I'm sure she'd be interested in evaluating the opportunities for your company."

3. **Not Having a Name Before You Call.** "We have been very successful helping improve the profit potential of businesses like yours. Whom should I talk with to describe the benefits of our cash management system?"

WHAT TO SAY TO THE DECISION-MAKER

Once you do get through to the decision-maker, your primary goal is to get his attention. Remember that he was doing something else before you called, so you must "steal" his attention away from that other matter.

1. **Deliver a Strong Opening Statement.** "This is Jane Jones from First National Bank. We're offering a payroll service to companies like yours that can save up to eight hours a week of clerical time. Would you be interested in gaining an additional day each week to focus on more important concerns?"

    Your opening statement should be clear and succinct and paint a picture of success for your prospect (see Table 9.3).

2. **Talk Benefits and Solutions.** Think in terms of what would be interesting and important to the prospect. The fact that you have a new product means nothing to your customer. It's only what your product can do for *him* that interests your customer. Your customers buy *solutions to their problems*, not products.

TABLE 9.3 Choose Your Words Carefully

Since you only have three seconds to make a first impression over the phone, the words you use are very important. Consider the following:

Motivating Words

"Will you help me?"
"Thank You!"
"Congratulations!"
"Please"
"You were very kind"
"I beg your pardon"
"It's been a real pleasure"
"I am looking forward to"

Probing Words

"What is your opinion?"
"What do you think?"
"Can you illustrate?"
"What do you consider?"
"What were the circumstances?"
"How do you feel about...?"
"What happened then?"
"Could you explain?"
"Why?"
"Oh?"
"Really?"

Irritating Words

"Understand?"
"Do you see?"
"Get the point?"
"That's not true"
"You are wrong about..."
"I told you..."
"Old friend..."
"I, me, my, mine"

3. **Use What You Know about the Prospect's Business.** The more you know about the prospect's business before you make a call, the better the call will go. There are many sources of information, including others in your company, newspapers, trade magazines, and community associations. You can also use

your knowledge of similar businesses to sell by reference. No one wants to be the first to try a new product. It's always easier to sell when you can refer to someone else who has already made the decision to use your company.

4. **Before You Pick up the Telephone, Set an Objective.** Ask yourself, "What am I trying to accomplish?"

By measuring your performance, you can see how you are doing and make the adjustments needed to be even more effective. Two common measurements to consider are:

Number of calls : Number of sales
Number of calls : Number of appointments

SUSTAINING YOUR MOTIVATION

Keeping yourself motivated is an important part of being successful on the phone. It takes persistence, and that takes an upbeat attitude.

Try these ideas for keeping yourself motivated.

1. Create a comfortable environment in which to make your calls. Sit quietly, away from the hustle and bustle. Relax, pour yourself a cup of coffee.

2. Reward yourself often for your performance. Set short-term goals, and give yourself small rewards when you reach them. Make it a game. "If I get through to ten people, I'll go for an ice cream cone after lunch." "If I get three commitments today, I'll buy myself a new cassette after work."

3. Publicize your success throughout your organization. Let others in the bank know how you are doing. Start a telemarketing column in the newsletter. Feed back successes to the branches, department heads, etc.

4. Ask for feedback from colleagues. Share your results and ask for tips. Get input that can help you become more successful.
5. Attend sales seminars to share ideas and learn from other sales professionals. Many other sales professionals use the telephone for selling. Tap into this resource.
6. Anticipate each call as a challenge. Look forward to stretching yourself. Expect success.

KEY IDEAS
WORKSHEET: TELEPHONE SELLING

1. How could you use the phone to save time?

2. What situations are you involved in right now that could be handled over the phone?

3. Look back at the opening statement you wrote in the Chapter 2 worksheet. Can you improve upon it? If so, rewrite it here and use it each time you pick up the phone.

10 Action Planning

Most people plan their vacations better than they plan their lives.

Mary Kay Ash

Even if you're on the right track, you'll get run over if you just stand there.

Will Rogers

Bankers are faced with many challenges in the years ahead. Ever-increasing competition, technological advances, and deregulation are changing the way you market your products and services. New consumer lifestyles are affecting the way you do business. You can no longer sit back and wait for customers. It is up to you to go out and find them (see Table 10.1).

This chapter contains a set of worksheets designed to help you put the information in this book to work for *your* success (see Table 10.2). Remember:

If it is to be, it's up to me.

" NOW THE BALL IS IN MY COURT. THE ONLY ONE RESPONSIBLE FOR MY SUCCESS IS ME. "

TABLE 10.1 How's Your Attitude for Success?

These are the attitudes for success. Can you answer yes to all of them?

Am I expecting the prospect to buy?
Will the prospect benefit from this product?
Will the prospect lose by not buying?
Am I talking with the decision-maker?
Do I have solid evidence to prove my claims?
Will I be able to answer his/her questions without bluffing?
Am I prepared to draw the prospect out with open questions?
Will I give up trying to sell after the prospect says no once?
Am I prepared to ask for a commitment: the sale or an appointment?

TABLE 10.2 Sales Affirmations

Use these sales affirmations to psych yourself up for success:

I believe in my products. I believe that they give people what they want.

My products solve problems and allow my customers to feel secure.

I am an ethical person; therefore, I am an ethical salesperson. I don't have to worry about negative opinions about salespeople; they don't apply to me.

I will start tomorrow on a successful note by making a sale today.

The purpose of my employment is to create new customers and develop those we have now.

I take a proprietary interest in my organization, just as though I were funding it out of my own checkbook. I can see how my sales contribute to its on-going success.

KEY IDEAS
My Major Customer's Needs

    Customer   Need

1.

2.

3.

4.

5.

6.

7.

8.

9.

10.

ACTION PLANNING

KEY IDEAS

Analysis of My Three Major Competitors

    Competitor   Advantages   Disadvantages   Exclusives

1.

2.

3.

What I'm Going to Do to Upgrade My Business and Banking Knowledge

1.

2.

3.

4.

5.

ACTION PLANNING 151

KEY IDEAS

My Sales Action Plan

"It's not what you *know* about selling that counts, but what you *do*." After reading this book, my two most important objectives are:

1.

2.

I'll take these five specific actions in the next thirty days to make sure I achieve my objectives:

1.

2.

3.

4.

5.

A CLOSING WORD

Now you're ready to go out there and sell. Every one of the ideas in this book *works*—but only if you put them into practice.

It takes persistence and commitment to be a successful salesperson. It takes daily practice of all the little things that add up to your professional image.

The time is *now* for you to prove what you can do. Good luck!

GLOSSARY OF TERMS

Cross-selling: offering another product or service to a customer who has agreed to one product or service.

Direct Mail: a letter or brochure mailed to a large number of prospects or customers for the purpose of creating awareness and/or making a sale.

Prospect: a potential customer.

Qualified Prospect: a potential customer who has stated that he will consider doing business with you, has a need for your services, and meets the requirements for those services.

Quota: the banker's sales responsibility defined in profit, revenue, total dollars and/or product units to be sold.

Referral: a name of a potential customer given to you by a customer, co-worker, friend, family member or associate.

Relationship Manager: a banker who handles all aspects of the customer's business with the bank.

Telemarketing: use of the telephone for selling.

Territory: the area in which the banker may operate his sales campaign, either geographic, by industry, business size or product.

Value: the customer's perception of the benefit received.

Appendix: Your Success List

BOOKS

Berry, Leonard. *Bankers Who Sell.* Homewood, IL: Dow-Jones-Irwin, 1985.

Carew, Jack. *You'll Never Get No For An Answer.* New York: Simon & Schuster, 1987.

Dane, Les. *Big League Sales Closing Techniques.* West Nyack, New York: Parker Publishing Co., Inc., 1971.

Fisher, Roger, and William Ury. *Getting to Yes.* New York: Penguin Books, 1981.

Garfield, Charles A. *Peak Performance.* New York: Warner Books, 1985.

Gschwandtner, Gerhard. *Quotes for Sales Success.* Fredericksburg, Virginia: Personal Selling, 1986.

Gschwandtner, Gerhard, and Laura B. Gschwandtner. *Supersellers.* New York: American Management Association, 1986.

Johnson, Spenser, and Larry Wilson. *The One-Minute Salesperson.* New York: William Morrow & Co., Inc., 1984.

Mandino, Og. *Greatest Salesman in the World.* New York: Bantam Books, 1968.

Micali, Paul J. *The Lacey Techniques of Salesmanship.* New York: Hawthorn Books, 1971.

Pennington, Judith A., *Creating a Sales Culture in a Community Bank.* Rolling Meadows, IL: Bank Administration Institute, 1988.

Richardson, Linda. *Bankers in the Selling Role.* New York: John Wiley & Sons, 1984.

Robbins, Anthony. *Unlimited Power.* New York: Simon & Schuster, 1986.

Waitley, Denis. *The Psychology of Winning*. New York: Berkley Books, 1979.

Waitley, Denis. *Seeds of Greatness*. New York: Pocket Books, 1983.

Ziglar, Zig. *Zig Ziglar's Secrets of Closing the Sale*. New York: Berkley Books, 1984.

MAGAZINES

The Philosophy of Success (602) 944-0248.

Sales & Marketing Management, Bill Communications, 633 3rd Ave., N.Y., N.Y. 10017 (800) 543-3000.

Success! 342 Madison Ave., N.Y., N.Y., 17173 (800) 234-7324.

CASSETTES

"Creating a Sales Culture," Barbara Sanfilippo.

"Sell Solutions, Not Products," Brunson.

The above tapes can be ordered by calling the Bank Marketing Association at (800) 433-9013.

"How to Deal with Difficult People," Dr. Rick Brinkman and Dr. Rick Kirschner.

"Listening," Lou Hampton.

The above tapes can be ordered by calling CareerTrack at (800) 334-1018.

"The Fine Art of Selling Different People Differently," Don Hutson.

"How to Use Telemarketing to Close Business," Sheila Bethel.

The above tapes can be ordered by calling the National Speakers Association at (602) 265-1001.

"How to Be a No-Limit Person," Dr. Wayne Dyer.

"Psychology of Achievement," Brian Tracey.

"Psychology of Winning," Dennis E. Waitley.

"See You at the Top!" Zig Ziglar.

The above tapes an be ordered by calling Nightingale-Conant at (800) 323-5552.

"Coaching Your Sales Team," Judith Pennington.

"Marketing Yourself in Your Organization," Judith Pennington.

"Sales Leadership for the 1990's," Judith Pennington.

"Selling to the Businessperson," Judith Pennington.

"Ten Secrets to Managing People," Judith Pennington.

The above tapes can be ordered by calling Pennington Group at (203) 740-2525.

"People Reading," Dorothy Leeds.

The above tape can be ordered by calling Organizational Technologies at (212) 864-2424.

"Time to Sell," Dr. Alec Mackenzie.

The above tape can be ordered by calling Dartnell at (800) 621-5463.